LORD, HELP ME WITH MY HYPERACTIVE CHILD

Evelyn Langston

BROADMAN PRESS
NASHVILLE, TENNESSEE

4260-64
ISBN: 0-8054-6064-0
Dewey Decimal Classification: 649
Subject Heading: Parenting/Hyperactive Children
Library of Congress Catalog Card Number:
Printed in the United States of America

All names in this book have been changed.

To Stacy

and the millions of other individuals
coping with emotional problems
or disordered personalities.

Contents

Foreword

The old Indian adage says, "I will not criticize my brother until I have walked a mile in his moccasins." The author of this book has walked many miles in the moccasins of those parents who must learn to accept and deal with a child who is less than normal.

Hyperactivity is a personality disorder that affects 5 million children. The untold pain and suffering that are caused by this malady would fill volumes. The immediate family, grandparents, other relatives, and friends are emotionally and physically impacted by the hyperactive person.

While society tends to joke about the person who is "hyper," those who must live with him or her find no reason to laugh. Hyperactivity is a serious abnormality and must be dealt with at the earliest possible recognition. Since there are so many facets to this ailment, there is no specific treatment or medication for all cases. Each individual must be evaluated and treated by a physician who specializes in this field of medicine. While medication is often a solution, it is not the final answer for every hyperactive person. Like Stacy, the subject of this book, many refuse to take their prescribed medications. This only intensifies the problem.

This is the story of one family's pilgrimage in dealing with this debilitating infirmity. It is for parents who have a hyperactive child. Grandparents, relatives, and friends will better understand hyperactivity by reading this book.

This book gives insight in the family turmoil that is caused by a hyperactive child. Those of us who have not dealt with this problem will gain knowledge about the disorder and find sympathy for the hyperactive person and his family. Those of you who have dealt with the problem will recognize that the author has walked in your moccasins. Those of you who are dealing with a hyperactive child will receive information about the disorder and suggestions about how to deal with your own emotional stability as well as your child's.

I have been more a front-row observer than a participant in this story. I have watched this family struggle through many valleys. Stacy has left them devastated many times. I have prayed with them and for them. I have seen the resiliency of their Christian faith. I have observed them practicing their beliefs when their moccasins were overwhelmingly battle-scarred. I have seen them win the victory and gain their dignity. Their story will encourage and bless you.

The story of Stacy is an unending one. This is true of most hyperactive persons. The conclusions of David and Angela Todd are biblically based. Though they are uncertain of future problems with Stacy, they have a plan of action that will help them deal with whatever problems may arise. They also have a Person who stands with them to help in every situation. Christ is the Lord of their lives and they have learned to depend on Him. They are confident that what they have learned, and the conclusions to which they have come, and the power of God are sufficient for any problem.

Read the book. Learn from it. Share it with someone else. All who read it will be helped.

E. RICHARD STEEL
Cedar Bayou Baptist Church
Baytown, Texas

Preface

Writing is an expression of my innermost feelings, which allows me to take a good look at myself.

I've grown spiritually as I have shared thoughts and Scripture passages with you. I have learned repeatedly to step out in faith, let go, open up, turn loose, and BELIEVE!

Through difficulties, I have learned that God's grace is sufficient to meet my needs.

Stacy, my hyperactive stepdaughter, was a shocking experience that let me grow and learn.

I didn't know what hyperactive meant when I married Stacy's father, but it only took a short time for me to realize how exhausting living with a hyperactive child is. I felt as though I was in the midst of a raging storm. Stacy was the storm! My hate, bitterness, and resentment toward Stacy became the elements I fought against.

God's love is more powerful than hate. Through prayer I learned to allow love to conquer my hate.

Travel with me through the stormy elements. Study with me the unique disorder of hyperactivity. Feel my frustrations and victories as a workable solution is found.

Acknowledgments

I'll never forget my typewriter breaking while I was in the middle of preparing this book. My youngest daughter said in a sarcastic tone, "I'm glad your typewriter doesn't work."

I realized then how demanding of my time this project had been. The constant click, click, clicking of the typewriter does sound louder and louder to those who must listen to it daily.

I became so preoccupied in writing that I often forgot to wash clothes, cook, or do any number of domestic chores expected of a wife and mother. When a hungry family said, "What's for supper?" and my reply was "Oh, is it time to eat?" I knew I had escaped unknowingly into the creative world of writing, leaving the "real" world behind.

My deepest love and thanks goes to my family for tolerating the noise and for coping with me while I endured the frustrations of a writer.

My genuine appreciation goes to Ann Sullivan, the creative writing teacher at Robert E. Lee High School in Baytown, Texas. Her advice and training techniques were wonderful and her contributions to this project were priceless. I'll always be grateful for her dedication, time, and abilities.

Jimmy Poepsel receives a very special thanks for assisting in the difficult and tiring chore of typing.

To many, many friends for prayers and support, I say thanks!

1

Portrait of *Stacy*

The warm spring sun beamed brilliantly through my bedroom window, gently waking me up. I snuggled under the sheets and hugged my pillow. I was wonderfully happy. The brightness and beauty of this morning reflected the love I felt for my precious David. I pushed the sheets away and looked out my window beaming my own ray of joy back to the sun.

I had been lonely and divorced for several years. Was it possible that I had at last found true love? David was a widower with two children: a six-year-old son and a twelve-year-old daughter. I had two daughters of my own, ages seven and three.

David and I had met through a mutual friend. We immediately liked each other and our friendship turned into a deep, meaningful relationship. Our dates were unbelievably romantic; they made me feel like I was floating away on a cloud. In just a few short months David and I were very much in love. A future marriage became our most talked-about subject.

I had not planned on falling in love, and definitely not with a man responsible for two children. I had been antimen for a long time. David had a way about him that made me realize all men were not the same. He was different and very special.

Our conversation about marriage was refreshing. The idea of being married took on a new vision of hope and happiness. I loved David, and I was sure I would be a wonderful wife and mother with his help.

I lay in bed a few more minutes, wondering what today would bring. We knew we wanted to get to know each other's children and give them a chance to become better acquainted with us. Today I would meet David's children for the very first time. I was a little nervous and hoped that they would like me. I stretched one last time, crawled out of bed, and began getting myself and my daughters ready for our monumental appointment.

David and I had planned a simple family picnic with the children. My daughters were thrilled over the idea of a picnic. They giggled and chattered all morning with the anticipation of the fun they would have.

My heart pounded when I heard the doorbell. I felt like I did at sixteen, all jittery and excited inside. I opened the door and there they stood. His little boy smiled sweetly and I remember thinking how nice it would be to have a son. I looked at Stacy and realized immediately that she was different. She looked somewhat like a tomboy, which was fine, though it was not what I was expecting.

I satisfied my curiosity concerning my first impression of Stacy by assuring myself that she was probably just a little immature for her age. David had never mentioned any deep-rooted emotional problems so I did not worry about the obvious immaturity that I had immediately recognized.

Introductions were made and we all felt the excitement of new friendships forming. We talked and laughed. I felt a sense of being complete.

The six of us loaded into David's car and drove off for our first family picnic. As we traveled to the nearby park, I could not help but smile as I listened to the giggling and talking of all four children. Stacy talked the most and and giggled the loudest, but I assumed she was just excited.

The park was beautiful. Spring is a wonderful time of year when the earth bursts out a freshness that always awakens my soul and excites me. I gazed at the beautiful azaleas, roses, and jasmines that were in full bloom. The flowers, grass, trees, sky, and birds seemed to sing a special song just for me on this beautiful day.

David found the perfect picnic location. He parked by a great big and handsome old oak tree. *That tree must be hundreds of years old,* I thought. It stood tall and proud and its branches stretched out in the form of an invitation. It was only a matter of seconds before each child had scampered up the beautiful tree.

"Look at me," they each said as if they were the only children in the world ever to climb a tree. "Yes, I see." My voice rang out in praise as I told them how special they were to be able to climb a tree that was so big. My few sentences of praise were not enough for Stacy. She called out for me to look at her at least a dozen times before David said, "OK, kids, keep busy playing so we can finish setting out the picnic food." The message was directed to Stacy and for the next fifteen minutes she played while we finished setting out the food, drinks, ice, napkins, and other picnic supplies.

Dating is such a special time for a couple, and I enjoyed the fun and excitement of dates with David. I was especially touched that David insisted on providing the picnic supplies to save me from the chore of cooking and preparing.

The aroma of fried chicken, potato salad, cole slaw and hot biscuits made all our mouths water. David had purchased our picnic at a fast-food restaurant, but I was not sure my home cooking would have been any better. Within a few minutes our table displayed a delicious Southern-style feast. We called the children around the table and David bowed his head and the rest of us immediately followed his example.

"Thank you Lord," David prayed, "for this wonderful day, this delicious food, the fellowship and fun, and for the miracle of love. Amen."

We all enjoyed our picnic meal. I had brought a chocolate pie, and a strawberry banana cream pie. I was gratified as the children made sounds of satisfaction while they ate the dessert.

After our meal the kids climbed the old oak tree again. While the children were preoccupied, David gently put his arms around me and hugged me. "You are the best thing that has ever happened to me." I gazed into his eyes and said, "I feel the same way." Suddenly it seemed like we were the only ones in the whole world. David held me closer and kissed me. "I love you," he whispered. "I love you too, David," I said.

Our romantic encounter lasted a few seconds until all four children began giggling in typical childlike manner. Our kiss was interrupted as a "time out" for affection. They hurriedly came down from the tree to receive their own kiss. The words "I love you" were exchanged and then everyone received a kiss and a hug. The whole loving scene was delightful and confirmed my feelings that we should join our families to make one big happy unit.

Stacy seemed to triple her activity after lunch. I had already been amazed at her high energy level, but now she had an extremely shocking amount of energy. She ran from one picnic table to the other, as if she was having a race with herself. She repeated this game over and over again. I could not imagine her endurance to such an exhausting game.

David and I were so involved in our own conversation and happiness that we did not pay much attention to anyone else.

We both noticed Stacy's abundant amount of energy but we did not place any importance on it. Neither David nor I felt a need to talk about Stacy that day.

It was obvious that Stacy needed more attention than the others. She laughed louder, was a little obnoxious at times, and talked at ninety miles an hour.

I satisfied my haunting feelings that something could be wrong emotionally with Stacy by convincing myself that she simply needed a mother. Losing her mother through death must have been devastating to her. That tragedy probably explained her immaturity. David mentioned that Stacy had been adopted at birth, so he was not aware of any personality traits that she might have inherited from her biological parents.

During the picnic, Stacy came to us often for hugs and affection. I was not sure why Stacy needed so much attention, but I was sure it must be connected to her sad past.

As I looked at the children, I realized that all of them suffered from a tragic loss, either through death or divorce.

My ex-husband had left, never to return. My girls suffered that loss and felt a sense of rejection. I really felt that the girls had experienced a tragedy as severe as a death might have been. Only time takes care of these heartaches. As time begins to heal our broken hearts, we hopefully begin to recover and put our mourning or disappointment in the proper place. This procedure takes time, and occasionally a little help in the form of therapy may be needed. I wondered it this might be the case with Stacy.

Our wonderful picnic ended and I found myself back home again. The house felt so lonely and empty without David and his children. My desire grew deeper for us to be married.

After baths and a number of routine activities, the girls and I went to bed. As I lay in bed reliving the events of the day, I thought about Stacy. I could not help but question why she had not adjusted as well as the others had. I wondered why she was so extremely active and talked constantly. I had never been around anyone who was always on the go! Surely her maturity would soon catch up with her age. I realized Stacy would present some problems and that I was probably facing a big adjustment. I was concerned about her overly affectionate nature and her nervous energy.

More than anything, I wanted to be David's wife. I knew our love would give us the strength we needed to solve any problem that might rear its ugly head. With that thought I went to sleep.

During the next few weeks David and I dated steadily,

involving the children in our social life as much as possible. Shopping trips allowed me some very important times with Stacy. I realized many things about her that seemed unusual to me. I was amazed at her lack of interest in cleanliness. Her teeth were stained due to neglect in taking care of them. Her hair had an oily texture, which is usually not present when routine shampooing occurs. Her young little body had an obvious odor, and I supposed it was because she played hard and did not bathe often.

I had not noticed these characteristics on the day of the picnic, but it was very noticeable now. These traits were signs of a low self-esteem. I wondered if it was somehow connected to her nervous personality. I grew just a little concerned as I began to question in my mind the extent of Stacy's emotional problem.

I decided to carefully mention some of my observations to David. He said he was aware of them, but I got the feeling they were not as disturbing to him as they were to me. He confessed he just did not know how to handle girls. So, once again, I dismissed Stacy's problems to the tragedy of losing her mother.

I truly felt I could help her and I looked forward to sharing my love with her. Maybe her abundance of energy just needed to be directed constructively.

Our spring was filled with love and happiness. Each day drew us closer to our June wedding until at last our glorious day had arrived.

My small living room was adorned with flowers and candles. David and his children arrived early so that we might go over last-minute preparations. Everyone seemed to overflow with excitement. Everyone but Stacy! She could not get her dress zipped and went into a panic. I was surprised that she had gotten that panicky over such a simple thing. We calmed her down, and were able to remove the thread that had caused the zipper to stick. She cried because her shoes made her feet hurt. I tried to keep her relaxed by assuring her that she would only have to wear them a short time. She picked at a small sore on her leg, causing it to bleed. I did not have any Band-Aids, so we had to make do with a tissue. Stacy seemed determined to be the center of attention no matter what! Even with all her annoying problems I was too happy to become frustrated with her.

Before long, our home was filled with family and friends. We all looked lovely in our beautiful new wedding clothes. Within moments our special time had come. We were repeating wedding vows. I heard the preacher say, "I present to you Mr. and Mrs. David Todd." Those words sounded wonderful to me. What a thrill becoming Mrs. Todd. I was now married to the man I loved so deeply. The air filled with laughter and talking. As I opened the wedding gifts, I noticed Stacy in the far corner of the room crying. A loving aunt was trying to console her, but it was not working. Finally David had to take her out of the room to comfort her.

That was the first time I remember feeling the bitter sting of resentment. She had been fine for months as she talked and laughed favorably about the wedding. Now it appeared she was sad. Of course, everyone noticed Stacy and felt sorry for her. They could only assume she was thinking of her own mother. I thought, *Stacy will do anything to gain attention and sympathy.* The other children were just fine, and I wondered why Stacy did not just dismiss herself from the group if she needed to cry. Why did she feel it was necessary to put a damper on our wedding? Was she jealous of my love for her daddy? I was deeply hurt by her display of emotion.

The other children knew Stacy well enough to recognize her ability to disrupt. They ignored her emotional dramatics and continued having a good time. This response from the children helped me to regain my composure. When Stacy realized nothing had changed because of her outburst, she shut off her tears and joined the others as if nothing had happened.

After the wedding, David and I left on a five-day honeymoon. David's children stayed with an aunt and my children stayed with my mother. We enjoyed our time together without interruptions. We called several times to check on the kids and they all seemed fine.

While we were so relaxed and everything seemed calm, I asked David about Stacy. He said that Stacy had always seemed different. He recognized her need for attention and said that she had always been hyperactive. "Hyperactive? What is that?" David looked at me with a shocked expression. "I assumed you could tell Stacy was hyperactive by her exaggerated level of energy." All of the sudden I felt stupid for having such a lack of knowledge. I did not know what hyperactive meant, but I was sure Stacy would do a very good job teaching me.

I had no idea what lay ahead of me, but I felt confident my determination would see me through.

2

Discipline for Our *Hyperactive Child*

Combining our families made quite a difference in our environment. Even healthy children cause all kinds of disruptions, but twelve-year-old hyperactive Stacy presented the challenge of my life.

Becoming a mother to four children was a little harder than I had thought it would be. It was a full-time job keeping up with the washing, cooking, cleaning, and other domestic chores that naturally belong to a household. I was continually amazed at the amount of dirty clothes and at how frequently they became dirty. Sometimes I felt like the children took clean clothes and put them in the dirty clothes just to punish me! Of course I knew they did not. I just could not comprehend the magnitude of the whole thing.

Buying groceries was a regular riot. I pushed two grocery carts around marking things off my shopping list, occasionally looking up to notice someone staring at me. I felt like I was buying for an army. I am sure it looked that way, too! Cooking for my big family became an art that took me months to master. In the meantime, I burned meals and broke dishes and I learned.

I went to bed each night totally exhausted. Each morning when the alarm rang, my body felt jolted from sleep. I managed to coordinate my brain, hands, and eyes to turn off the alarm. As I dragged myself out of bed, I felt like I was waking up to a new dimension in sound. My ears were bombarded by an endless array of noises. Kids yelled because socks, shoes, and belts could not be located. Accusations were slung from one end of the house to the other. I had never heard so much noise in all my life, and Stacy made more noise than all of the others put together.

Accepting the new challenges of motherhood was a hard job. Stacy added something to my being a mother that I was not fully prepared to handle.

I was familiar with the typical fussing, fighting, tattling, giggling, and being silly that is to be expected from normal, energetic children. Stacy's actions and noise levels were exaggerated, extreme, and something entirely new to me. Her enormous energy was unbelievably ceaseless and left me feeling as if I had received a charge from a lightning bolt. Stacy's extra energy found expression as she added a jig to everything she did. Brushing her teeth involved marching, twisting, and turning. As she combed her hair, she danced. The fork became a drumstick at the dinner table. Watching television included swinging her leg, biting her fingernails, and picking her nose. She rubbed her arms and legs and scratched her face in a nervous rhythm. She hummed as she wiggled her fingers and toes. The excitement she experienced while laughing caused coughing episodes which resulted in even more noise. Stacy was so active I felt like she climbed the walls and hung from the light fixtures. She did not just flip her foot during a tense moment, she did a complete dance routine from sunup to sundown.

My day started out like a keg of dynamite exploding! After a number of outrageous explosions, the kids were finally gone to school, and the house became suddenly quiet. It was clear that my new life with David would not be all fun and games.

One morning at nine o'clock the phone rang, quickly snapping me back into the real world. It was Stacy's English teacher. "I'm sorry to bother you, but I'm at my wits end with Stacy. She has disturbed the class every day this week. She continually talks and laughs even when I ask her to stop. I actually had to turn her desk to the wall so the rest of the class could study!"

Suddenly I felt sick. What had I gotten myself into? I assured the teacher we would take care of the problem even though I did not have the vaguest idea how. I hung up, and immediately the phone rang again. It was the school dietitian. I was aware of the school policy to assist children who forgot their lunch or lost their lunch money.

The policy allowed a charge to be made so the child might be able to each lunch in such a case. A notice of this school policy had been sent home to inform us that our children might take advantage of this school benefit if they needed to. I was not worried about Stacy using the charge system because making a lunch for four kids everyday was as routine as drinking my morning coffee. I was shocked when the dietitian told me that Stacy had charged $25.00 worth of food.

The dietitian was calling because the notices sent home by the school had not been signed and returned. Stacy ate the lunch I prepared for her then charged anything extra she wanted. She told the dietitian she had forgotten her lunch.

I just could not believe it! First of all, Stacy knew she was not suppose to charge any food because I had given her a lunch. Second, she was dishonest about showing me the notice the dietitian sent home for me to see. Finally, she had lied to the dietitian about the reason she was charging the food.

I was embarrassed and wondered what in the world the dietitian must think. She probably did not know who to believe. I told her that I sent a lunch to school with Stacy. Stacy told her she did not have a lunch.

This seemed to be one of those mornings that refused to go well. My sick feeling turned into nausea. The lump in my throat began to ache and I just sat down and cried!

Stacy's attention span was remarkably short. No wonder the English teacher felt a sense of hopelessness.

Stacy had no stick-to-it power, no ability to follow instructions or finish tasks. Even completion of simple tasks seemed to present too much of a challenge for Stacy. Homework remained incomplete. Preparing for any activity seemed impossible. When she dressed she forgot to brush her hair and teeth without being reminded.

Stacy was like a tornado, whipping though our home, causing all kinds of damage and destruction in just a matter of minutes.

At times Stacy's problems seemed too big for me to handle. Maybe it seemed so big because there was not an immediate solution. My common sense told me the answer consisted of patience, tolerance, endurance, and constant control. I knew what the answer was, but following through was a different story. Just the thought of it all was exhausting!

This day had been too much. I cried for hours. I felt like I had arrived at the bottom of my pit. I felt sorry for myself and spent hours wallowing around in self-pity.

Being the Christian I am, it was not so unusual that I turned to prayer and Bible study. Many times I found peace through prayer when I was struggling with a particular problem. At this time, I found myself more or less begging for some kind of explanation from my Heavenly Father. When I opened my Bible for comfort, I turned to 2 Corinthians 12:7-9. "I have placed this thorn in your side for a reason. It will allow you to grow in strength and depend on me. My grace is sufficient for thee: for my strength is made perfect in weakness" (v.9, KJV).

Somehow I just was not ready to hear how a painful thorn was going to cause me to grow. I remember saying, "God, I have had so many thorns during my life. Are you sure this is the only way I can grow spiritually? I do not want an irritating old thorn to contend with!"

I knew for a fact that God had taken my trials and troubles in the past and allowed spiritual growth. *It is a shame I cannot grow without having to go through a trial,* I thought.

My only hope was heavenly help and I knew it. There was no way I could face this raging storm that brewed inside Stacy twenty-four hours a day all alone. I needed the supernatural strength God would give to me through prayer.

When David came home from work, I told him about the school problems. He was surprised, but he did not express the same shock I did! I had reacted with horror at Stacy's uncontrollable behavior at school. I had never experienced such frustrations with a child. David mentioned that Stacy had presented school problems before. I was appalled at David's calmness over the situation. I paced up and down the floor nervously, rattling on and on about how she must learn or *else!* I had no idea how to handle Stacy or the situation, but I was angry, and thought David should be too. My first instinct was to beat Stacy half to death and teach her to *never* be disruptive again! That, of course, was not realistic.

I watched Stacy's reaction in amazement as the facts were presented. She screamed at the top of her lungs that the teacher lied. "I didn't do that," she yelled. My mouth flew open. I could not believe her denial. I walked over to the phone and said, "Well, maybe I misunderstood. I will call your teacher." She screamed and stomped around saying "No! No! Don't do that!" She began crying hysterically, as if she might not take her next breath. I stared at Stacy as she continued her dramatics. Stacy then changed her tone of voice and the sound level of sobs and said softly, "Why don't you believe me?"

What a scene! What an actress! She really deserved some kind of award for such a superb performance. First she denied the truth, and then she tried to make us feel guilty for not trusting her. She actually believed her extreme efforts would convince us she was right and the school authorities were wrong!

Trying very hard to maintain control, we hoped to help Stacy accept responsibility for the wrong she had done. We decided to use an old-fashioned disciplinary action, the spanking. It worked. She settled down and we gained control. The spanking was administered hard enough that she would remember the punishment; however, it was not so hard that it was abusive in any way. Four to five firm swats with the belt did the trick. We said, "Stacy, you cannot go through life doing what you want to do. There are rules to follow and when you choose to break those rules you must suffer the consequences. These spankings hurt, so next time think before you do something you are not supposed to do!" She cried as if she had been beaten unmercifully.

Stacy's memory was not the same as that of a typical child, and many of our teaching techniques had to be repeated over and over again. Consistency became the key word. Spanking is not usually necessary for a twelve-year-old child. By that age, children have usually learned to do what is expected of them. Of course Stacy's maturity level was that of a much younger person. In order for spanking to retain its effectiveness, we used it as a last resort. It was saved for the "biggies." The school difficulties with the English teacher and the dietitian were considered *big*.

Stacy had temper tantrums when she did not get her way. Those tantrums became a little less frequent when she realized we would follow through with a spanking. It was not unusual for her to scream, kick, and stomp around if someone spoke to her in a way that displeased her. A spanking provided the control we needed over the situation.

Meanwhile, my patience was still lacking. I obviously was not praying hard enough for my heavenly strength.

My temper flew almost as loudly and dramatically as hers did. She screamed, then I screamed back, and for five minutes or longer, we exchanged screams. I look back on these scenes shamefully. I certainly was not growing spiritually, and until I gained more patience I was headed downhill. Matters could only become worse when I added to her temper tantrum with my own uncontrolled feelings. It was important that I learn to assert my authority without becoming hysterical. I reminded Stacy that we were the parents and she was the child. I also reminded myself that I was indeed an adult and should act like one.

Stacy had temper tantrums over the smallest things. She lost control if a comb or a piece of jewelry was misplaced. She was panicky if she asked for a snack thirty minutes before a meal and I told her she must wait until after the meal. She screamed at the other children if they disturbed her in any way. She cried over any disappointment. If the disappointment was big she sobbed uncontrollably. If an insect happened to crawl by, she screamed as if she were frightened to death.

I began checking out books about hyperactivity in order to learn all that I could about Stacy's disorder. Stacy's symptoms were so pronounced that I easily identified many of her characteristics as those listed in the books.

In my research I discovered that most hyperactive children have short attention spans and demand to be the center of attention. Hyperactive children generally feel an itchy sensation on their skin, which explained Stacy's constant scratching.

Researching the subject was very helpful. I began to wonder why Stacy's disorder had been ignored. I asked David why Stacy was not on medication. He admitted that he and his first wife simply did not put much emphasis on her high energy level. She was the only child for years and they excused her behavior thinking she was just unnaturally active.

Finally, I was acknowledging resentful feelings toward David and his first wife. I was very critical and thought to myself, *What kind of mother would let work dominate her life so much that she was too tired to recognize serious symptoms such as Stacy's?* I tried to avoid these ugly thoughts and focus on the present, knowing there was not one thing I could do about the past.

Reading the Bible was always a comfort, especially when I was confused, hurt, and swamped with negative thoughts.

James 3:1-2 says 'Dear Brothers, don't be too eager to tell others their faults, for we all make many mistakes. . . . If anyone can control his tongue, it proves that he has perfect control over himself in every other way" (TLB).

It was clear after reading the Scriptures that I should not be so critical, even in my thoughts. I was not involved in the situation at that time, so how could I be sure what I would and would not recognize?

David and his first wife had planned to have a family, but after ten years of trying unsuccessfully they adopted Stacy. Six years later a surprise came with the birth of a son.

Unfortunately, David's wife became very sick and was diagnosed as having cancer. Her sickness demanded all of David's attention and energies. Stacy's disorder became worse. David's preoccupation with his wife's illness caused him to unconsciously avoid Stacy and everyone else.

David remembered Stacy's behavior during the time her mother was ill. He said she seemed very unconcerned that her mother was sick. She might have appeared unconcerned simply because she did not know how to express herself. With an unbalanced system she was not able to show her feelings. Stacy's only desire seemed to be owning a pet hamster. She asked for this pet so often that she became a nuisance. David had to become firm with her many times when he tried to explain that she could not own a hamster because of the danger a foreign object would have on her sick mother.

When Stacy's mother passed away, Stacy appeared to not have been affected at all. Here again, actions can be deceiving as we remember Stacy's body was off balance. When the funeral was over, Stacy looked up at David and said, "Now, at last, I can have a hamster." David was totally frustrated, hurt, disappointed, and angry with Stacy's uncaring attitude. He never purchased the hamster. He was too grieved to understand Stacy's silent plea for help. Stacy took a turn for the worse.

I felt sure I could help guide Stacy in the right direction. Little did I know how big the problem already was.

Stacy had four strikes against her: She fought rejection from her biological parents, she was unable to understand or accept the death of her adopted mother, she was extremely hyperactive, and her disorder had been unattended to because of unfortunate circumstances. Being hyperactive is confusing enough, however, it can be controlled through medication, diet, and therapy. It was very unfortunate that Stacy was not given the help she needed at an early age.

Stacy certainly was not the typical child, and even though she had a reason for her emotional problems, we would not excuse her uncontrollable behavior. We could not allow her to control us: we must learn to control her.

I thought of the very inspiring story of Helen Keller. It was unfortunate indeed that she was the victim of a very serious illness. She was ill from a high fever called brain fever. Because of this, her sight and hearing were destroyed before she was two years old.

There have been a number of plays, movies, and books written about Helen Keller, and her remarkable teacher Ann Sullivan. An established fact is that the first five years of Helen Keller's life were spent undisciplined. She expressed herself by kicking, scratching, uttering the choked screams of a deaf-mute, and was plainly out of control.

When Ann Sullivan entered into Helen's life she taught her through discipline. When she established authority, then Helen responded: She learned to read Braille, write, and eventually speak.

Helen Keller is an outstanding example of a person who conquered physical handicaps, and was willing and able to teach and encourage many others. She was literally helpless without the teaching and discipline of Ann Sullivan.

Helen Keller did not ask for her unfortunate circumstances, but she was able to make the best of a bad situation through the tools of love and disciple.

Stacy did not ask for her unfortunate circumstances either. My deepest desire was to help teach her through discipline and love.

According to the books written about Helen Keller and Ann Sullivan, it was necessary for Ann Sullivan to be stern. Even though Helen's parents were appalled, they soon learned this firm approach was the best.

I thought of this illustration because I felt guilty when it was necessary to spank Stacy in order to gain control over a situation. It helped my feelings as I realized it would benefit her in the long run.

We used a number of other approaches including time alone in her room, a privilege taken away, a written report assigned to explain reasons for correction, or writing a number of sentences. For example, "I will not tell a lie because it is important to be honest and trustworthy," a hundred times.

Love became part of the discipline. Our love prevented us from allowing not only Stacy but any of the children to continue in a poor behavior pattern. Our love urged us to try everything possible to help redirect those poor manners. It was important that each of our children heard the words *I love you*. We repeated those words often during the day.

Each child heard those words before discipline was administered. We felt this expression of love was very important.

This expression of love was especially important in Stacy's circumstance. She lacked reasoning. At times she did not understand what she had done wrong and she felt she was not loved any longer. A little explanation saved emotional hurt and confusion.

In most instances, Stacy was sent to her room to write a summary of what she had learned from the experience. This served two purposes: It gave her time to settle down in the solitude of her room, and she was also forced to consider the events that resulted in punishment. We took advantage of the quiet time to settle our own anxieties. Discipline that worked for the other children was not as effective for her. Whatever form of discipline brought the desired results was applied.

I was discovering that *love* and *discipline* were key words as we raised Stacy.

3

Reactions from the Family

I learned from reference books in the public library that hyperactivity is caused by a biochemical imbalance that affects the child's entire system. Five million children have been diagnosed as having a hyperactive personality disorder. I can not help but think of the number of mothers, fathers, sisters, brothers, relatives, and friends who are affected by the problems of these children. Adjusting and learning to live with this powerful force requires a joint effort.

Being a parent certainly had its difficult moments. Becoming the stepmother of a hyperactive child might not have been as devastating if I could have seen some progress or sensed some positive response from Stacy.

I wanted to be a good mother, loving and sensitive to each child's needs. Painfully, I realized I could not offer Stacy a precise cure.

Anyone can become a housewife. Cleaning, organizing, planning, and cooking are a matter of choice and discipline. Becoming a good mother involves listening, teaching, loving, talking, understanding, caring, and just being available. That may sound easy, but every parent knows that it is not. I wanted to become the best mother I could possibly be. That desire became the biggest challenge I ever accepted.

At times I felt I was being stretched to the breaking point! Adjusting to Stacy seemed impossible. Somehow, I had to learn to cope with Stacy and still make time for my other children. I often found myself worked into a frenzy because I was torn emotionally with a feeling of pity and sympathy for Stacy. My common sense told me she could not help herself. At times I felt anger toward her, and at other times I was overcome with compassion for her as she struggled to become part of the group. These mixed emotions caused serious difficulties.

Perhaps Stacy hysterically tattled that her brother or sisters did some horrible thing to her. Before I even gave the other child an opportunity to explain, I responded to Stacy's hysteria, made a quick judgment, and scolded the wrong child. My own stress blinded me.

I specifically remember a painful episode that clearly showed me what I was doing wrong.

A Southern summer is very uncomfortable. The heat alone can drain your emotions. My ability to rationally cope with the children had slowly dwindled during the hot month of June. By the middle of July I was literally counting the days until school started again.

I had provided many activities for the children such as trips to the library, swimming at the Y.M.C.A, picnics, and visits to the zoo. I was trying very hard to be a wonderful mother. Three children enjoyed the activities I planned and showed appreciation for my efforts. Stacy, however, appeared to hate any activity no matter what! She whined and complained about every situation.

Stacy had a terrible habit of going though our personal belongings. Many times I found her in our bedroom, looking through drawers and closets. When this situation occurred, she was grounded to her room for a period of time.

On this particularly hot summer day, the air conditioner was broken and we were all miserable. The heat had created stress in all of us. The summer heat and fussing from the children caused me to be extremely nervous.

Stacy was riding her bike around the neighborhood and the

other children were playing. It seemed each child had come in or out of the house every five minutes. It was cooler under a shade tree than it was in the house, but boredom caused anxiousness in each one of them.

I went into our bedroom and discovered the five-dollar bill I had placed in my little money box was gone.

I was already a nervous wreck, drained emotionally from the heat, and sick to death of summer, kids, and fussing. Discovering my money was gone made me furious! I instantly assumed one of the children presently in the house was guilty. I stomped in the living room and hatefully demanded for the children to "Come here now!" I was sweating and my face was red partially from the heat and partly from being upset.

Firmly, I asked, "All right, who took my five dollars?" Not a word was spoken. "Have it your way," I said. "You will all stand in a corner until someone confesses."

I assigned a corner for each child and then I went back into my room feeling like I would surely die from overexposure to children.

I waited and waited for a confession, but it did not come. Finally after about thirty minutes, I heard a soft voice say, "May I come in please?"

"Yes," I said. I could not believe my oldest daughter had come to me. I did not know who took the money, but I was almost sure she had not.

My daughter said, "Mom, why are you punishing us? You know down deep in your heart we did not take the money."

I looked at her tenderly, then burst out crying. I called for the other children to join us, and I tearfully apologized to each one. My heart felt like it was literally breaking in two. Yes, I did know deep in my heart who took the money.

We spent the next hour sitting on my bed sharing frustrations that Stacy created. The confession was a wonderful release for all of us and we enjoyed the support we felt from each other.

Stacy's bike ride usually lasted several hours. Her absence was such a relief that I did not really care how long she was gone. The extra activity seemed to balance her overactive system for a short time.

When Stacy did come home I noticed her wallet. I stepped up to Stacy and firmly said, "Stacy, let me see your wallet." I was steaming mad, but I remained in control. Instinct must have told Stacy not to argue. My expression was probably interpreted as "destroy." I was proud of the fact that I did not scream, yank, jerk, or cuss. I looked in the wallet, and there was the five-dollar-bill.

"Stacy, you have deliberately stolen from me. You will pay the consequences for this choice." I said. I then gave her four swats with the belt and sent her to her room to write a report on "why it's wrong to steal."

I looked at the other children compassionately as my eyes filled with tears.

"Children," I said, "parents are not perfect, and I am doing the best I can. Please forgive me for punishing you when it should have been Stacy."

They expressed sympathy for me as they, too, emotionally battled with Stacy's disordered personality.

I realized I needed to provide time for myself, away from the children, without interruptions. My nerves were demanding peace and quiet.

I found a quiet place to meditate and pray. I prayed for a new awareness to the problems around me.

During this quiet time I began making new commitments. It was clear to me that my body and brain were stressed to the limit by noise and confusion. Among my decisions were:

1. To provide more time for myself, away from the children.

2. I would pray more often. Prayer is the power source of all Christians. It was my loss when I did not take advantage of the benefits that belonged to me as a Christian.

3. I would spend more time with each child personally.

The visit would be for one child at a time to provide an opportunity to recognize that child's feelings.

4. I would distract each child into a specific area that highlighted and developed their natural abilities.

My new commitments proved to be an excellent growth time for mother/child relationships. Each child felt special because of the individual time I spent with them and they anxiously began to share their special hopes, and their worst frustrations.

I began to pray for each child separately as well as spend more time in prayer for my own self.

It is I who drift from God; not God who drifts from me. What a shame I let the activities of day preoccupy me to the extent of leaving out my visits with God.

The children loved it when I joined them for lunch at school. Elementary years are so special, and I realized there would be a time in their teen lives that they would not want this kind of fellowship with me.

I found my children were very talented. Our boy loved sports, while the younger girls loved ballet and choir. Stacy enjoyed band and R.O.T.C.

In my efforts to direct each child, I began to feel like a taxi driver. Voice lessons, dance practice, and athletic workouts became routine events. I chauffeured each child to his or her respective practices and each child took pride in their special activity. The driving time provided an opportunity for a meaningful conversation.

Stacy did not cause disruptions on purpose, but no matter what, we all had to learn to handle the five to ten disruptions daily that she did create.

A disruption was fussing, tattling, pouting, and being unwilling to do what the rest of the family wanted to do. We could count on them! It is hard for even an adult to contend with such disharmony. It was extremely hard for our children to cope.

At least once a day we could count on an explosion! An explosion was more extreme than just a disruption. It consisted of screaming, crying, extreme rudeness, and a temper tantrum. No family is perfect, nor is any person. My continual talks with God certainly did give me extra strength and coping power. I found if my prayer life was not continual, my impatience was displayed more quickly. I could feel that my prayer life was adding to my abilities to endure the situation much better.

Coping became a daily challenge for each family member. We all learned to avoid certain situations. Other situations seemed just impossible to avoid.

One very painful lesson for me to learn was how to handle criticism more constructively. David had a problem in this area, too. We simply could not think of doing things any other way than our own way. When we grew angry toward each other, matters became worse.

Many problems stemmed from Stacy's noncaring attitude towards cleanliness. Stacy often stated she had taken a bath but there was seldom any evidence of cleanliness when she came out of the bathroom.

David and I then argued among ourselves whether she did or did not bathe. Stacy appeared to enjoy the upset between us, which created even more friction. In most cases we were very supportive of each other and tried to avoid arguing in front of the children. When our nerves and emotions were raw from the many upsets we endured, our lack of understanding and communication were temporarily destroyed.

Something as simple as questioning Stacy's bath was usually not argued over. David or I generally instructed Stacy to bathe again if she did not smell fresh or if her hair was still oily. When arguments came too often, our ability to rationalize the situation was less tolerable.

My emotions always leaked out through my eyes and I cried. Never, in all our years of marriage, have we ever gone to bed without solving our differences. That one simple rule saved us from many long-drawn-out fusses and enabled us to solve the problem faster.

I loved having David's big, strong arms around me. I always felt so secure when he hugged me. David reminded me many times that we could not allow Stacy and her problems to destroy the love we felt for each other.

At times I even resented David because he went to work and I stayed home. It seemed to me that he escaped most of the turmoil by going to work and I often wished I could escape from the house nine to ten hours every day by going to a job.

Working out of the house, however, was not the answer for me. I was afraid to go to work. The children were too old for day-care and I did not feel I could trust anyone to come into my home and try to manage what was so hard for me. I knew Stacy would cause disruptions and explosions and I was not sure how an outsider would handle these problems. Thus, it seemed that the only sensible thing to do was to learn to handle it myself.

When problems occurred too often, my anger ran out of control, and I could not think straight, I knew it was time for a break.

David and I were aware of each other's need to get away from the friction. It was obvious that neither of us could face such distractions for long periods and remain mentally healthy and sensible. About three times a year I visited my mother for a week. David took over the job of mother and father for that week so I might have the opportunity to regain my emotional strength. When I became emotionally drained, I was not worth much. During these times I felt like a person wandering helplessly in a dry desert. My food, water, and supplies were all used up. My trip away for a short time was like stumbling upon an oasis. It refreshed me and renewed my inner being. The rest and relaxation were a must. I was able to return refueled and ready to start again. I could face the challenges that awaited me daily with a better attitude.

Even though David had always taken an active role in helping with the children, it was not the same as the full-time role he was forced to assume when I went to my mother's. He, too, fell victim to increased anxiety as he was constantly forced into uncomfortable situations with Stacy. Our seventy-five-pound ball of fire brought out the worst in both of us! David always showed a new appreciation for me when I returned home after a short vacation.

In all fairness, it was only right to be understanding when David needed a fishing trip away from it all. When he returned home, I greatly appreciated his contributions as a "daddy" much more.

An important fact was for us to share in the responsibility together. Neither of us could carry his load alone. Each needed to lift the other up. We were in this together.

4

Medication Can *Help*

Research helped me understand the "whys and hows" of Stacy's problematic world. Understanding the problem was the primary ingredient for coping with the problem.

It was interesting to find that hyperactivity is also referred to as hyperkinesis, minimal brain dysfunction, impulse disorder, and many other terms. "Hyperactivity" is defined by doctors as an excessive and uncontrolled activity within one's movements. Hyperactivity, in many cases, is identified with the central nervous system, as well as emotional stress. Many hyperactive children develop psychological problems resulting from rejection by peers. Their race-car personality irritates adults and drives away friends of their own peer group. They are categorized as problem children who constantly cause disturbances in the classroom and other functions. Their behavior is inappropriate, and learning problems emerge because it is literally impossible for them to sit still and learn in traditional ways.

Doctors agree that medication can be a tremendous help. Medication will not solve all the problems, but after the medication slows down their system, psychological problems can be more effectively treated. Psychological problems refer to attitudes, self-esteem, reasoning, and understanding.

Research concluded that a child does outgrow a hyperactive nature. There is no magic age for this to take place. The child may be as young as twelve but could be as old as eighteen or twenty. Psychiatric help may be needed to aid in the reconstruction of the child's attitude.

Brain disorders are revealed in different ways. Hyperactivity is one of those ways. Doctors have confirmed that the electrochemicals which control body activities have been altered. The result is excessive movements by the muscles.

Our saddest experiences with Stacy resulted from her refusal to take medication. Our doctor prescribed Ritlin to be taken three times a day. We personally watched her take the morning dosage and I even asked her to open her mouth so I could see if she had swallowed it. It was up to her to take the other prescribed dosage while at school. This medicine was vital. It would have slowed down her system enabling her to sit still and concentrate, providing an opportunity for learning to take place. We asked daily if she had taken her medicine, and she always said she did but we recognized her exaggerated responses and irritating mannerisms so we knew she could not possibly be taking her medication.

We were saddened when we found large numbers of pills hidden in pockets, lunch sacks, and other places. In her mind, the medicine classified her as mentally sick. Our pleading did no good at all; she never understood the importance of taking her medicine.

Taking only the morning dosage was like washing greasy hands with a thimble of water.

I often wondered what changes might have occurred if she had regularly taken the correct dosage. She developed a hit-or-miss approach, which did absolutely no good at all. We were so involved in trying to slow her system down that the psychological problems grew out of control.

I realize now that there were other approaches I could have taken. I could have made arrangements for her to come home for lunch, enabling me to administer her noon dosage. I wish now that I had discussed the situation with the school nurse.

The school nurse normally oversees medicine taking at school. This could have been the answer.

My attitude at the time was this: "Why do I have to spoon feed Stacy like a baby? Why should I rearrange my whole life for a child who simply does not care about her own self?" My bitterness prevented me from helping Stacy reach her full potential. This was a crucial mistake on my part. I asked myself continually, "What if I had done this or that?" Sometimes our choices as parents can be tragic. Hopefully, sharing my mistakes will motivate any actions necessary to make sure your child takes his needed medication.

At the time, I was not willing to admit that I could have made any changes. I felt like I was doing all that I could do, and it was Stacy who was not willing to make a change. The fact is that Stacy was chemically off-balance which hindered her rational thinking.

5

Suggestions for *Parents*

I made it through each passing school year. I was learning answers to some problems and there had been improvements in some areas. My marriage had not been exactly what I envisioned it would be on that summer day in June when I married David. In spite of the fact that these kids kept our lives filled with problems, I was still very much in love.

Loneliness is an awful feeling of emptiness, and I still felt I had made the right decision.

One problem that never seemed to change, even with time and acquired patience, was summer. For me, summer was like an awful black cloud that slowly settled over our house. I started dreading summer during the children's spring break from school. During that one week, with all four children home at the same time, I was reminded how awful summer would be. I cried as I realized the school year was coming to an end. It was difficult enough to face all the children every day after the school day was over. In just those few hours remaining before bedtime, there were many disruptions.

Each summer I felt like I was in the middle of a hurricane and I was amazed how these children had the ability to completely wipe out my emotions. I felt bitten, chewed, swallowed, and spit out. There are really no words that could adequately describe my drained sense of emotions.

A nervous twitch developed. Sometimes my mouth lost its entire shape and stayed wide open for minutes at a time.

Some other times I just sat and stared at the wall. My ears were unable to completely tune into all they were hearing. Ridiculous sounds bounced around the room like a rubber ball. The sounds never made sense, they just made an awful noise. I kept hearing sounds like, "Stop looking at me," or "Your foot is on my side," or "I'm telling!" The summer months were extremely hard, and very trying. When summer was finally over it took months for me to rebuild my tolerance level.

Stacy's hyper nature added tremendously to the stressful summer. It was even hard to find time to escape to the bedroom for a quiet time of prayer. One day I decided to try to regain my composure by slipping off to my bedroom. I collapsed onto the bed saying to myself, "if I could just take a little nap I would be fine." I did not realize what a courageous effort this would be. As I lay trying to sleep, one child decided to type, one child was playing the piano, one child became involved in an Atari game, and the last one sang at the top of her lungs.

I came roaring out of my room screaming, "All I wanted was a little nap!" They looked at me like I was crazy.

I am not sure when children become thoughtful. I am not really sure if they can even comprehend an adult's need for quiet. I suppose at one time I thought children were just born with the need to be considerate! What a joke!

The longer I tried to conquer the task of raising three energetic children, and one very hyperactive child, the more I realized that children have an instinct to blame someone or something when they are caught displaying bad manners. I heard numerous times, "He made me do that," or "She told me to do that." It seemed impossible for the child to say, "I'm sorry, I know that I did wrong. I'll try to remember to do better."

Anytime problems occurred in Stacy's life, we heard this remark: "They're mean to me, they aren't my real parents."

I am not sure what that implied. David was certainly the only father she had ever known and I tried hard to be the best stepmother. I heard the statement, "I'm adopted," so often that I realized there was a deeply rooted insecurity within Stacy. I always thought that adopted children would feel special, knowing they were handpicked. This is not so and my research revealed that many adopted children feel insecure.

These insecurities within Stacy made it more difficult to teach her simple things about manners. She interrupted, talked too loud, laughed too hard, and asked inappropriate questions. She never understood why these manners were unacceptable.

In my efforts to teach the children manners, it seemed that they would comprehend some things part of the time and then at other times I would feel that they never heard a word I said!

I was always researching. It helped and I seemed to find satisfaction in studies that offered some form of hope.

I realized both parents and children make choices which cause consequences. How can a child learn if the parent rescues him from every mess in which he becomes involved? We all have lessons to learn and mistakes to make. I am so busy making my own mistakes and paying my own consequences that I do not have the time or energy to pay for anyone else's mistakes.

I know of parents who continually suffer because of their children's decisions.

The following paragraph is from an article I received from our school district. It was very helpful to me. We tried diligently on many occasions to teach Stacy by allowing her an opportunity to experience the outcome of her wrong choices. She did learn in some areas, while in other areas she did not. These guidelines helped me tremendously with the other children who did not lack the chemical balance Stacy needed.

FOUNDATION FOR GOOD DECISION MAKING

To develop good decision making skills in children:

- Provide an atmosphere in which children can make choices.
- Be consistent in allowing children to make decisions.
- Respect children's choices.
- Encourage children when they work at good decision-making skills.
- Consider what decisions are appropriate for children to make at different ages.
- Help children consider alternatives and outcomes.
- Allow children to experience the outcomes of their choices.
- When children make a poor choice, allow them the opportunity to make other choices at a later time.

Not all hyperactive children established a lying pattern. Many psychological problems develop due to the reaction from peers so that any number of problems may exist.

Stacy's hyperactive nature had certainly created psychological problems and a pattern formed where lying seemed to stand out. It became one of the strongest problems. She did not learn from her mistakes and developed an ability to act out lies. Many, many times she lied her way through a conversation. When she was caught in a lie, I was amazed at her ability to continue to lie, even though we were presenting to her evidence and facts! A good example of this is the illustration of Stacy's denial to the schoolteachers and dietitian's complaints. It was very clear that Stacy had turned into a habitual liar. She told new lies to cover the old lies. Her lies became a snowball, growing in size every second. Amazingly, she seemed to have remarkable control. Her expressions were sincere, with not even a trace of fear due to the lie she was telling. The list of lies grew long and unbelievable. She lied when it was easier to tell the truth. Her lies caused more stress for David and me to cope with. She lied about where she was going and who she was with. When she was involved in school fund raisers, she collected money, spent it, and then lied saying someone stole it.

Many hyperactive children develop the ability to lie and this appears to be a typical problem of hyperactive children. We learned to double check Stacy's stories. If she was not where she was supposed to be, we approached her with facts. In most cases she became outraged because we were "spying on her." We calmly announced that as parents we had privileges. We reminded her that she had given us reason to doubt and that it was up to her to earn that trust back. We told her repeatedly we would check on her and she would face the consequences for lying. Routinely, when Stacy had permission to go somewhere, we said, "You know we will check, be where you are supposed to be and learn from your mistakes."

Silently I wondered if God would ever remove the painful thorn in my side. I questioned if I was learning from all of this. I knew my character would show its strength according to the way I handled my problems. I continually prayed for the ability to endure.

Stacy was extremely intelligent. Unfortunately there was also a severe lack of motivation. This too was another psychological problem created from hyperactivity.

We tried different approaches to keep Stacy interested. She was given the privilege of taking night courses at our local college. At first she responded well to the challenge of a more detailed study; however, she lost interest after a short time.

Stacy read some of the many books made available to her concerning hyperactive children. We asked for a written or verbal report to insure us that she understood what she had read. This little home study offered Stacy insight into understanding the mechanism of hyperactivity.

One interesting viewpoint was in the book by Fiengold *Why Your Child is Hyperactive*. Dr. Fiengold is an eminent allergist and pediatrician. His advice has been helpful to many. He believes the behavior disturbances and learning disabilities in hyperactive children are caused by artificial food flavors and colors.

Some parents have successfully controlled their child's emotional outrages by controlling their diet. We tried and failed in this area, too. With an extreme effort we were able to control Stacy's diet at home, but while away from home she ate what she wanted. Here again, we have an example of the hit-and-miss theory. I never understood how Stacy could have knowledge of her problem and still choose to avoid correctional methods.

I asked our doctor this question. He replied by saying that the dieter also has knowledge of what makes him or her fat, but chooses to continue putting into their mouth those foods that they know will add to their miserable weight problem. I thought this was a very good illustration, and I understood with this example. The doctor used other examples like the alcoholic, the compulsive spender, and on the list goes of the many problems that exist because of an undisciplined nature or emotional problem.

I suppose we will never know what makes some able to overcome their problems, while others allow problems to overcome them.

The "blaming game" seemed to apply to us. We blamed Stacy for not making the right choice. Stacy blamed the teachers, and the teachers blamed us. A better communication link was needed. We found these things helpful:

1. Teacher conferences,
2. Telephone calls to continue good communication,
3. Exchange of parent-teacher notes.

Even with these efforts Stacy's behavioral problem continued. Her talking, scratching, clicking, thumping, and laughing went on uncontrollably. Academic problems on top of all the psychological and hyperactive problems created a disastrous situation.

As Stacy struggled through each year of school, I, too, struggled right along with her. I made it a point to keep up with her progress. Most of my conferences with teachers only added more discouragement to my already heaped-up pile. I felt like I lived at school. Things seemed so hopeless. Stacy completed junior high school by a close margin. Her theory became "Why study if I can still pass without studying?"

High school brought new hopes as well as new problems. Stacy had been in the band all during junior high and seemed to really enjoy the activities and fun events that the band offered. In high school Stacy continued her efforts, but she was too clumsy to march during the Friday night football games. Every week she went through the ordeal of practice marching so she might qualify to march in the game, but she was never able to qualify. The band had many projects and field trips. We allowed Stacy the privilege of going on these trips. When the trip was over, I usually heard from an exhausted parent or teacher pouring out complaints on Stacy's poor behavior.

We handled the complaints in different ways. Most of the time she lost the privilege of going on the next trip.

After losing money for the second time, she was not allowed to participate in fund raisers any longer.

We had high hopes when Stacy became part of the R.O.T.C. program which was an organization offered to those students who are considering a career in the military. We desperately hoped she could follow through with this possibility. This organization offered many activities that required self-discipline in some way or the other. Stacy, however, could not follow instructions or remember what to do after she heard the instructions.

I continued every effort to create an interest in home projects since Stacy was left out of so many high school activities. I longed for her to be able to participate like the others. How come she did not learn from her mistakes? The consequences were always so hard on her.

One of the biggest affairs of high school was the annual homecoming football game. The girls all hoped they would be invited to the homecoming dance celebration after the big game. The boy traditionally gave the girl a beautiful homecoming mum corsage. On homecoming day, the girls all delighted in wearing their beautiful mums to school. I could not stand the thought of Stacy not having one, so every year I bought her a beautiful mum. She seemed thrilled! I hugged her and said, "Just tell everyone that a real nice friend gave it to you." That certainly was the truth. I was almost Stacy's only friend. Of course, no one had to know the mum was from her mother.

When Stacy finally became a senior, I had hoped she would be able to participate in some activities with the band and R.O.T.C. simply by learning from her past experiences. It seemed that things never improved and she continued her pattern of not being able to follow instructions. No matter what kind of consequences she suffered for poor study habits, lying, or unacceptable behavior, she continued presenting problems.

A phone call from the school informed us of a strong possibility of Stacy failing her senior year. As a parent I had a desperate need to frantically share and explain all we did to help Stacy. I felt embarrassed to be associated with such a problem child. I knew the harsh judgments of most people would assume that her behavior was a reflection of her home life. Realizing this, I felt the need to share with the school counselor all we had done in an attempt to help Stacy.

"We encourage, we give praise, we teach responsibilities, we follow through with discipline, and we are consistent in hoping she will learn," I said. "We give her nice material things. We are doing all we can. We are good parents!"

I was almost crying at this point. I had accepted the challenge of raising Stacy, and I had given that challenge my best effort. I wanted the counselor to recognize my efforts since these efforts certainly were not recognizable in Stacy. I shared a final personal story with the counselor in an attempt to satisfy myself that he knew we had done everything possible. The story was about the time we surprised Stacy with a party that I created just for her in an endeavor to help her feel loved and wanted. I called it an appreciation party. I had a cake made that said "We love you and appreciate you." I sat it on the table with several gifts placed around the cake. We hugged her and told her how very much we loved her. She was surprised and expressed appreciation for these efforts. By the next day her attitude seemed the same as it did before the party. I told the counselor that I was not sure I believed the old saying "Love can change anything." I had loved my heart out and it had not seemed to change a thing. By this time I had began to cry. I had sincerely, genuinely, given Stacy all I could give, but she had rejected me and my love.

With a kind voice the counselor said, "If Stacy refuses to accept her disorder, refuses any kind of professional counseling, refuses to take her medication routinely, then there is nothing else you can do." He continued, "You are looking for a change but there will not be one. The chemicals in her system must have medication to help her become a balanced person."

The disappointment I felt was overwhelming. The counselor continued, "Take a firm stand and do not allow her to disrupt your life and the rest of your family's lives." I almost burst out laughing. Unless we sent Stacy to a foreign country there was no way she could avoid disrupting everyone's life that she came in contact with. The secret would be learning to endure her extremely disordered character without losing our own minds.

I realized it was important to talk with someone who offered understanding and I appreciated the words of the school counselor.

This conversation took place around the middle of Stacy's senior year. I felt like I still had time to persuade Stacy to study. I knew I could not just stop trying even though the counselor said not to expect a change.

I found the biggest comfort and relief for me was in sharing with my pastor. Talking provided valuable input from him and allowed me an opportunity to release my stress and tension. He continually prayed for me and offered many suggestions grounded on biblical truths. I knew there were situations in life that I would have to accept because some situations are unchangeable. I began to feel that Stacy was very possibly a condition I could not change. Even though I drew my strength, love, and peace from God, that did not mean that Stacy did. I could not make Stacy lean toward heaven for help. I could not make her love God, nor would God force His love on her, either. Stacy had to come to God on her own.

A Bible verse that my pastor shared with me was Colossians 2:6-7. "Since you have accepted Christ Jesus as Lord, live in union with him. Keep your roots deep in him, build your lives on him, and become stronger in your faith, as you were taught, and be filled with thanksgiving" (GNB).

These verses meant a lot to me. I would strive to keep my roots planted in Christ, and become stronger in my faith. My faith would see me through. I would continue to study and seek the wisdom of others who were knowledgeable about hyperactive children. I would continue every effort in hopes that some day, somehow, one of my neat ideas would work. I would continue to review material and books that offered suggestions and an insight into Stacy's problem. I could not give up. I had to continue trying.

I found the list of suggestions the school counselor had given me very helpful and often reread them.

SUGGESTIONS TO PARENTS OF HYPERACTIVE CHILDREN

1. Keep colors soft.
2. Keep voices low and gentle.
3. Avoid explosions.
4. Learn from mistakes.

5. Be consistent in discipline, praise, and encouragement.

6. Have a routine schedule.

7. Avoid negative words and negative responses.

8. Supervise medication times and stay in close communication with your doctor for possible changes in medicine.

9. Share helpful hints with schoolteachers.

10. Examine the possibilities of therapy.

11. Educate yourself to a better knowledge of hyperactivity.

12. Become familiar with nutritional suggestions and recognize what foods and artificial coloring affects your child.

13. Direct your child toward a possible future career.

14. Make stands to avoid crisis.

15. Develop harmony with your other children and your spouse.

6

The *Hasty* Way

My new involvement with Stacy's disability generated an interest in other handicapped children. With a new interest emerging I was amazed at how much more aware I became of those children suffering with handicaps around me.

We all have handicaps of some kind, but many, many children and adults suffer from severe handicaps. I began observing individuals and became amazed at how well some overcame their problems and how poorly others handled theirs.

Meeting special people can be a priceless gift. I felt very fortunate to become acquainted with Ruth Hasty. Ruth Hasty is the author of *How to Teach Dyslexics and Other Nonreaders*. I met her through a friend who taught junior high school. When my friend began telling me about Hasty's book, I called the author. She was gracious enough to set aside a time when we could talk. Ruth Hasty is a successful teacher. She taught science and music for eleven years. She developed a special interest in children and adults who could not read. Ruth Hasty spent the next twenty-two years studying and working with nonreaders.

Ruth Hasty realized how hopeless nonreaders felt. That realization challenged her to overcome obstacles and develop techniques that offered help for an overwhelming problem.

I was fascinated as she shared her teaching efforts that effectively taught children to read, write, and spell, who otherwise could not.

I was amazed when she stated that many dyslexic students were also hyperactive.

She said, "I had to slow way down in teaching dyslexics. I modified and expanded my program. I started out intense and then backed off."

Hasty said that at times teaching children with learning disabilities became very frustrating. "I had to learn to keep on keeping on. I taught the hyperactive children that just because they were hyperactive, they were not excused of poor behavior." She explained, "I used a short-term approach for hyperactive children. I started trying to teach them to sit still for five minutes, then I built on that."

Ms. Hasty taught at Colorado State Hospital for three years. The hospital was equipped to handle patients ages twelve to eighteen on a short-term program. She said, "I was very impressed at the percentage of children who benefitted from this program. The program offered counseling, therapy, education, and met every type need the child had. Of course, not every patient profited. Some left the hospital just as disturbed as when they came."

Hasty talked about the expense of a program with a criterion that met physical, psychological, and educational needs. "It's expensive," she said. "When I taught there, it was twenty to thirty thousand dollars a year for long-term patients. Insurance programs paid for a large percentage, as well as government assistance for those who qualified."

Ms. Hasty is very knowledgeable and has researched areas of disorders in individuals for years. She had attended and profited from many seminars associated with behavioral problems. At one of these seminars she asked the instructor, a doctor, a very interesting question; "Why is it that some problem children can handle difficulties while others can not?"

"Choice," the doctor said. "Some individuals choose not to make the very best of every situation. Some children want to learn and some children think they have to have things their way." He continued, "Rebellious children are harder to teach and some of them choose to never pay attention and learn. As adults these individuals are still rebellious and stubborn."

I was fascinated by Ruth Hasty, the ability she had, and the patience she acquired qualifying her to teach difficult students. Hasty said, "The human brain has marvelous powers and with the right teaching, can overcome tremendous obstacles."

She emphasized being pleasant and patient. "You get much better results if you are nice, smile, and stay pleasant." Being pleasant and consistent are vital. These same teaching techniques can be applied to many children who struggle with a disorder.

It was obvious to me that Ruth Hasty was a gifted teacher. Her teaching techniques were the key that opened the door for many nonreaders.

Many of Hasty's insights were developed through training her own handicapped children. Ruth Hasty's first child suffered with polio but had a brilliant mind. "She was reading the newspaper at four and asking questions at six." She told how she became very depressed over her daughter's illness. "I almost lost my mind!" Ruth's husband began telling her how she would be unable to help their child if she could not overcome this depression. "I made up my mind at that time that there would just be one patient and not two!"

Her second child was a slow learner. "I was so confused. One child was brilliant, and one child could not learn at the average pace. He was in the fourth grade before he could read." Each child had a different handicap and each child had different needs.

"They are self-sufficient adults now. My daughter is an editor for a small newspaper. She still continues to overcome obstacles because of her lame legs but she has accomplished this daily challenge very well. My son is the custodian at a junior school."

I thought this information was marvelous. Even though her children were handicapped, creating all kinds of difficulties, they both maintained an adult standard of living and were responsible for themselves.

Sharing with someone this knowledgeable and experienced gave me a broader understanding of children with learning disabilities.

Ruth Hasty said, "I can always tell who ate what during lunch. Junk food and soda pop seem to make hyperactive students more active. I dread lunch time."

Many doctors, teachers, and instructors have differing opinions over the same research material concerning food. My own research was forcing me to consider every aspect.

Today had been special. I was excited to learn about so many new ideas and approaches—the Hasty way!

7

Working on *Confidence*

Children can be terribly cruel. Unfortunately, Stacy became the victim of many hateful remarks from other children. Her hyperactive personality disorder was so overpowering that insensitive children took every opportunity to make fun and ridicule her.

It is not uncommon for hyperactive children to lack confidence. Stacy's low self-esteem manifested itself in many ways. Her posture was slumped at all times, and her head hung down low. Her walk was a mixture of shuffling and marching. She never noticed if her clothes were buttoned wrong, zipped crooked, or if her dress was ripped. She continued to be unconcerned if her face was dirty, teeth neglected, or hair oily from lack of shampooing. Stacy had a nice wardrobe, but whatever she put on reflected her feelings of a poor self-image.

There was never a time that I knew of when Stacy was interested in keeping her hair and body clean. Daily baths and shampoos were required, but she just sat in a tub of water getting her hair wet to show the appearance of being shampooed. Her hair lacked bounce and glow. Her body continually had a hint of odor. This one area in personal hygiene caused many quarrels. It was beyond my wildest imagination why anyone would choose to look sloppy and smell bad when there were other choices.

With much persuasion, I convinced Stacy to try some beauty secrets. We went to the beauty salon where they gave Stacy a simple shampoo and set. I felt the beauty treatment idea would be just the motivation Stacy needed. The beautician was appalled at the condition of Stacy's crusty scalp and oily hair. I was so in hopes that as Stacy heard these concerns from someone new, it would change her attitude.

When someone saw Stacy's awful appearance it was embarrassing to me. I tried hard to encourage her to look nice, but she just did not care. Stacy was not a reflection of her environment, and I knew I must learn to swallow my pride and ignore rude looks. There was no way I could explain the situation to anyone.

Stacy looked up at me with an awful expression on her face. I could tell she did not like her hair. I thought it was beautiful. Maybe she thought the difference in her appearance would create more attention than she already received. I do not know why she did not like her clean, bouncy, glowing hair, but she did not!

I connected the low self-image and sloppy appearance as being part of the same problem. I wanted to help Stacy so much, but Stacy had to first want to help herself.

Confidence is the most valuable asset to an individual. Many disabilities may occur but with confidence so much can be achieved. My thoughts drifted and I remembered how much I enjoyed watching the Special Olympics. Many of these children have unfortunate mental and physical problems. Their ability to accomplish a difficult task is very inspirational.

I longed for Stacy to have the determination that other children had. Many times I had encouraged her to watch the Special Olympics hoping she might feel some inspiration from their determination.

My thoughts had taken me away from the present moment. Once again I looked at Stacy, only to be disappointed by her mad expression.

After the hair care was completed a skin specialist gave

Stacy a facial and applied makeup. The specialist gently advised Stacy of the consequences of neglecting her skin.

When the beauty treatments were complete, I was amazed at the difference in Stacy's appearance. She really looked pretty. She, too, finally seemed impressed. Her hair glowed and bounced with body and curls.

Her face radiated with a beauty that only makeup can capture. I took pictures when we got home. I wanted to remember this day forever. I felt sure this was the beginning of something wonderful. Stacy seemed excited about her new appearance and I was so pleased with myself for thinking of such a terrific idea.

I quickly had the pictures developed, but in the meantime Stacy had slipped back into the same sloppy rut. When I showed her the pictures she was pleased but styling her hair and applying makeup seemed to be too much trouble and took too much time.

I was just sick! I could not believe this experience at the beauty shop had not changed a thing. I had been certain that if Stacy saw for herself the difference in her appearance she would change her desires. I was wrong!

I continually fought those nagging, embarrassing moments when Stacy looked awful and people stared at us.

I did not offer Stacy any compassion during times like these. My own embarrassment dimmed my desire to be sensitive towards her. This was my own ugly weakness shining through.

Stacy's senior year grew close to an end. As an end of school activity the R.O.T.C. planned a special trip out of town to visit a military base.

Stacy was extremely pleased that she would be able to attend this activity. David and I were a little apprehensive but felt the trip would be a great experience.

A week before the trip Stacy was extremely hyperactive, but I did not think much about it as I realized it was due to the excitement she felt in planning an out-of-town trip. Any child experiences a surge of excitement when special activities are planned.

We helped Stacy with packing and organizing so she would not forget any essential items. We also encouraged her to take her medication.

I took Stacy to school on the day of the field trip and hesitantly said good-bye as I watched the bus pull away. I wondered if Stacy could be gone for two days without presenting any problems.

The Air Force base was located 200 miles from school. The group of students left on Friday and would return Sunday evening.

The house seemed wonderful quiet and we were not too concerned about Stacy. She was seventeen, soon to be eighteen. We hoped that this would be a growing experience for her.

The R.O.T.C. teacher seemed to be understanding and patient which added to our hopes that the trip would be successful.

When Stacy returned home she appeared tired. She talked to us a few minutes and then unpacked her things. After a few nighttime procedures she went to bed.

David and I looked at each other. David said, "Something has happened." I also feared the same thing. Stacy's short conversation and lack of enthusiasm indicated that somehow something had gone wrong.

Our suspicions were confirmed the next day. The R.O.T.C. teacher called from school. He started the conversation by saying, "I regret to inform you that Stacy will not be allowed to attend any more trips with the R.O.T.C." With an opening like that, I knew I had better sit down for the rest of the conversation. He said, "Stacy never slowed down from the second she got on the bus until the time she arrived back home."

The more the teacher talked, the more his voice was that of a very angry man. It seemed that retelling his experience with Stacy made him even more angry. He said, "She never followed one rule, nor was she where she was supposed to be even once! All activities had to be delayed until we could locate her. We were late to each function because we had to stop and find Stacy." I was speechless. I did manage to mumble out an "Oh no." The teacher said, "The worst of Stacy's actions was the way she followed every boy and man around! One time we found her with a boy she hardly knew. I was shocked to see how freely she displayed her affections!" I could feel my face burning with embarrassment and my eyes misty with tears.

The teacher ended the conversation by saying that Stacy became so excited as she watched the military men play a basketball game that she hyperventilated. The teacher seemed to express humiliation in his voice as he told how he had to stop watching the game and take Stacy to the first aid station.

After Stacy was given a bag to breathe in, she was able to regain control. The teacher told us that this was the worse experience he had ever had with any student in all of his twenty years of teaching. I felt so bad. I wanted to say something to make things better, but what could I say? Of course, I apologized for Stacy's actions, but why was Stacy not able to realize her actions were inappropriate? She did not even know how annoying she had become to others. What was there left for us to do? A spanking, grounding, or request to write a report had only provided temporary changes in Stacy's behavior.

My thoughts were not able to escape the fear that gripped me. Would Stacy ever be able to function on an acceptable adult level?

I cried the rest of the day to release some of my painful tension. When David came home from work and I told him how many disruptions Stacy caused in two days, he was also deeply disturbed. Our thoughts were the same. *What in the*

*world would we do with such a powerful force within our
lives after school was out?*

During my sobbing and weeping, I prayed, "Oh God, have
you left me? Why can't I teach Stacy?"

Suddenly I thought of 2 Corinthians 12:7-10. These Scriptures were about Paul to whom I felt so close. His painful
thorn paralleled so well with my trial. I read the scriptures
once again.

*"A messenger from Satan to hurt and bother me, and prick my
pride. Three different times I begged God to make me well
again. Each time he said 'No. But I [Christ] am with you; that
is all you need. My power shows up best in weak people.' . . . Since
I know it is all for Christ's good, I am quite happy about 'the
thorn,' and about insults and hardships, persecutions and
difficulties, for when I am weak, then I am strong. The less I
have the more I depend on him" (TLB).*

I was not sure I was going to be as happy as Paul was about
his hardships, but I was sure this difficulty had taught me to
lean on the Lord much more than I ever would have without
my painful situation.

As I closed my Bible, a little poem fell out that I had saved
for years. The author was unknown and I can remember
thinking what a perfect time it was for me to reread it. The
poem truly gave me strength.

The Weaver

My life is but a weaving
Between my Lord and me.
I cannot choose the colors.
He worketh steadily.
Oftimes He weaveth sorrow,
and I in foolish pride
forget He sees the upper
and I the underside.
Not till the loom is silent

> and the shuttles cease to fly
> shall God unroll the canvas
> and explain the reason why.
> The dark threads are as needful
> in the Weaver's skillful hand
> as the threads of gold and silver
> In the pattern He has planned.

Trusting God was easy to say and hard to do. I seem to fail over and over again. I had to simply step out in faith and turn loose of my fears. Why was that so hard for me to do?

I knew deep down in my heart God would give me the strength I needed. I was not sure what the outcome of this situation would be, but what ever it was, I had to have faith that God would be with me.

8

Anger *Exploding*

I always took pride in my abilities to adjust to a difficult situation. I was a positive person and felt that there was a solution to every problem.

My determined attitude stemmed from the many difficulties I was forced to cope with during my life. My childhood taught me to handle the problems that a mentally ill father presented. I suffered with a low self-esteem for years, which made me appreciate the importance of confidence.

I married a military man at the age of nineteen. I was saddened to find he had multiple emotional problems which resulted in an unhappy marriage. My father committed suicide when I was twenty.

I lived ten years in a miserable marriage that consisted of moving from one military town to the other until my husband divorced me. I struggled through financial problems and a lonely existence for years. Only through God's love, guidance, and strength was I able to survive such heartaches.

When I met David I was thrilled to find true love and happiness. Even when I recognized that Stacy would be a problem, I felt sure my abilities to successfully overcome difficult situations would help me to achieve success with her and her problems.

David and I had been married for five years now. Our marriage was a success because of our strong love and our willingness to communicate. Stacy presented some gigantic obstacles but we always managed to work around her problems.

After the R.O.T.C. teacher shared his devastating experiences with Stacy I became even more concerned about her future.

If Stacy could not function in an acceptable manner for two days, what would she be like on a continual daily basis? High school occupied hours of her time. Without those required hours of school she would be at home with me. Just the thought of her presence all day long was more than my mind could handle.

My body began to show the stress it had endured for so long. I could always tell when I had not gone to God for strength because my body shouted out in pain.

My body showed its stress when I began to walk, talk, cry, and scream in my sleep. It seemed at this particular time I had forgotten all about my faith and had fallen into the worry rut again. I was extremely nervous and on edge.

David also suffered because of stress. He began experiencing chest pains, and his blood pressure became high. It was necessary for him to take medication in order to control his high blood pressure.

Here is a clear and very vivid illustration of what can happen when you are not fueled with prayer.

My thoughts dwelled on directing Stacy into a lasting future that would provide her security and absence from us.

After hours of thinking I decided we could possibly invest in a small frame house or mobile home for Stacy to live in after she graduated. I knew if I located something inexpensive it would still be costly for us since we were living on an average income. I analyzed that without Stacy's many problems, our nerves and our children's nerves would be better than the emotional strain we were experiencing.

I spent the next several weeks searching for some kind of suitable living quarters for Stacy. I found a small, old house for sale that was advertised at a low cost. I became excited when I saw the house. I realized how easy it would be to fix up and make it suitable, keeping the cost to a minimum. I became even more excited with the thought of Stacy being gone.

I was, once again, proud of myself for thinking of such a neat idea. I could hardly wait to share my thoughts with David. Three children were watching television and Stacy was bike riding. I asked David to join me in the bedroom so I could present my wonderful plan. I noticed his expressions were not exactly what I thought they would be. I was shocked. He finally exploded, shouting all kinds of negative remarks at me. His eyes grew big and his face became red with anger. He shouted, "This is great! You are going to just kick my kid out in the cold!"

My mouth dropped open and I said, "I hardly think I am kicking her out! I have tried for five years to help her."

Then David said loudly, "So after five short years you are giving up?" I could not believe my ears. David was aware of the stress our family experienced because of Stacy. Where did this negative response come from? I explained the reasons I felt this change would be good for all of us. It would give Stacy the opportunity to be independent. She could get a job and pay her utilities and buy groceries. If she was unable to keep her job because of her inability to follow rules, she could become part of a job placement program. I had investigated and found that programs were established for individuals lacking motivation. Most importantly, our family would be free of the large burden she placed on us. I knew we would still visit her, and keep up with her progress. We just would not experience the same burden of her continuous presence.

I was amazed at David's attitude. It was if he was not willing to admit Stacy had a problem. He continued speaking loudly for about an hour, informing me that Stacy was not our only problem. He said, "You act like if we get 'rid' of Stacy there will not be any problems!" I was so hurt. I had been calm up to this point, but now I was mad.

"How dare you talk like this?" I screamed. Then I began to cry and between sobs said, "She is our only problem. I have given my very best to that child and she still has not made any changes. I have changed though! I am a nervous wreck!"

David did soften his voice just a little and said, "How would you feel if I moved your girls out of the house the minute they graduated?" Then he said, "You can never understand how I feel because you have not had Stacy for eighteen years."

I looked at David and realized the conversation must end. David looked at Stacy through different eyes. I saw her as a problem child who would never change and David saw her as a child who was a little immature but who would change in time.

Our fuss lasted for hours and the children heard us screaming at each other. It was not the only time the children had heard us fuss, but it was the only time they had heard us fuss for so long and so loudly. The youngest child broke out into a frantic cry saying, "Please do not get a divorce, please do not get a divorce!" With that expression of fear from a child, our fuss ended. We tried to comfort each child. We felt sorry that they had witnessed such a scene. Stacy had been riding her bike most of the time but she, too, was aware that we were fussing.

I was glad the children were not aware of what the fuss was over.

The argument ended, but anger continued to rage inside of us. David was outraged that I wanted to "get rid" of Stacy. I was outraged that David was not willing to change our stressful situation.

The Christian life is not easy. Life is never perfect whether you are a Christian or not! As a Christian I felt like a roller coaster going up and down in my spiritual life. Sometimes I remembered to pray for strength and avoid upsets. Other times I did not. Sometimes I felt mad at everyone, including God. Most of the time I at least recognized my weakness and could pray for strength and understanding. It is true that life is hard no matter what, but life was at least easier to cope with because of the strength God provided.

Even though I was a slow learner, I could see that my trial was in the process of teaching me patience. I was a little further down the road than when I first started and I felt that I had obtained some patience.

Someone has said that Americans pray like this: "Lord give me patience, and I want it right now." Charles Swindoll said that it is awfully hard for a country that exists on frozen dinners, instant mashed potatoes, powdered orange juice, packaged cake mixes, instant print cameras, and freeway express lanes to teach its young to wait.

9

A *Survival* Kit

Even though David and I continued to talk and do routine things, the hurt we both experienced showed in our silence and through the expressions on our faces. It would have been foolish to refuse to discuss our feelings. After a day of not talking, I went up to David. As I looked at him we both said, "I'm sorry" at the same time. It felt so good to hug each other and be able to discuss our feelings without being misunderstood. It was very clear that we had a difference of opinion. It was also clear that we loved each other very much. Neither was willing to let the other go.

We did not know what the answer to the problem of Stacy was, but we were willing to try other possibilities. We made a new commitment that day and began to think of some ways that might guide Stacy in a new direction.

Stacy had received psychiatric help once when she was about ten after her adopted mother died. She responded so bitterly to counseling that her counseling sessions were discontinued. Many years had passed and we felt it might be helpful to try again.

I realized Stacy's psychological problems were already deeply established. If we were able to convince Stacy to receive counseling, it would probably take years to unfold what was so well established in her mind.

When we confronted Stacy about going to a psychiatrist, she stomped, screamed, and cried. She said, "If you take me to a psychiatrist it will be because you hog-tied and dragged me in!" We asked the psychiatrist what we should do and he said, "Without Stacy's willingness to cooperate, counseling will be useless." We decided to wait and in the meantime we would continue to try to convince Stacy that counseling was necessary.

I was in hopes that one day soon she would agree to counseling and when she did I wanted to be ready. I realized how costly therapy was, so I educated myself about the fees and how arrangements could be made. I found that some insurance plans would pay up to 80 percent of the total cost. In other situations, arrangements can be made through a monthly payment plan.

Again I found myself saddened because Stacy had not been on therapy and medication at an early stage. I continued to think that early medical treatment would have been an answer.

It was hard not to see how my stress was gnawing away at my nerves. When talking, walking, and screaming in my sleep continued, David realized how serious my problem was. He made arrangements to allow me more time alone. I appreciated his thoughtfulness.

He stayed with the children twice a month on Saturday while I took the day off and escaped from the house and Stacy. I took advantage of this time and did a number of things that provided relaxation and aided in releasing my tensions. I often went to the Y.M.C.A. which provided hours of fun. The gym was great for jogging or walking around; also for shooting baskets and playing volleyball. My Saturday outing became a wonderful event that I looked forward to. It allowed me a tremendous break and gave David a closer insight into what was going on. I felt it was important for David to understand the full impact of my stress. My Saturday outing offered David closer involvement in family operations. This recuperation time allowed me the opportunity to look deep inside myself. I could always see things more clearly if I was not

stressed to the limit. I realized that I had become somewhat
of a nag. I could talk of nothing else but the kids and how
horrible Stacy was. No wonder David reacted the way he did
over my suggestion of moving Stacy.

I took advantage of my quiet time and used part of it to pray
and ask God for strength.

Sometimes I felt like I was getting worse instead of better.
Proverbs 27:15-16 came to my mind. "A constant dripping on
a rainy day and a cranky woman are much alike! You can no
more stop her complaints than you can stop the wind or hold
onto anything with oil-slick hands" (TLB). I am sure I fit in
there somewhere. There were certainly days I could have
been compared to a constant dripping! Other verses in Proverbs brought awareness to me. "Self-control means controlling the tongue! A quick retort can ruin everything" (13:3;
TLB) "A soft answer turns away wrath, but harsh words cause
quarrels. Gentle words cause life and health, griping brings
discouragements" (15:1,4, TLB).

When David and I were first married, we exchanged love
notes quite frequently. He often found a note when he opened
his lunch container at work or under his pillow or taped on the
bathroom mirror. Somehow through the years our note passing discontinued. I knew that these little notes were a great
uplift for me and for him, too. So, I began to reestablish this
fun habit; it was refreshing and gave me the encouragement I
needed. David had always taken me on dates. This time alone
gave us an opportunity to enjoy each other's company in a
special way. I looked forward to these dates and it was just
what we needed to confirm our love. Holding hands, hug-
ging, kissing, and doing sweet things for each other were the
little things that helped us survive.

As we reconstructed our survival kit, we remembered how
important our communication with each other was. After the
big fuss that exposed our raw feelings, we realized our communication needs might be a little more demanding than

those of other marriages. We became more sensitive to each other. I listened more to David and he listened more to me.

At the end of the day I sat in the kitchen trying to collect myself before he came home from work. When I had a bad day it was very apparent as it showed in my actions and my voice. David lovingly looked at me and asked, "Did you have a bad day, Honey?" Sometimes I just burst out crying, other times I managed to say weakly, "I made so many mistakes, I had to give myself an 'F.'"

David worked hard and I am sure my frustrating day was not what he wanted to hear the minute he came home from work, but he patiently sat down and listened as I poured out every detail of my horrifying day. I talked and talked and talked until I felt better. David listened patiently and at times he added helpful suggestions. This was part of my survival kit. David provided this therapy for me. I needed this time to talk and express my disappointments of the day. David was more patient than I was, but occasionally I had the opportunity to listen to him release his anxieties.

Thoughtfulness determined how well our survival kit worked. David surprised me one night on a special date. He arranged for us to have a romantic dinner and then afterwards he handed me a beautiful diamond and sapphire ring. I was thrilled.

David and I wanted our marriage to be successful and the thoughtful things we did for each other would see us through.

No matter how much research we did on the subject of hyperactive children, we always wanted to read any new books we might discover. Two books that benefitted us were: *The Hyperactive Child and the Family* written by John Taylor, PhD., and *The Hyperactive Child* by Dennis P. Cantwell, M.D.

These books, so full of knowledge, were priceless to our understanding. John F. Taylor writes:

Your child may lack insight into the hyperactivity and may deny that he is hyperactive. Among the abilities that hyperactive can impair is the ability to make social judgments, including judgements about self. Your child may be psychologically blind to his own hyperactivity. Hyperactive children are almost always confused and surprised by the negative reactions of others because they do not recognize anything irritating in their own actions. Your child's traits must be acknowledged by you without upset.

Statements like this from Taylor reminded us that Stacy's actions were caused unconsciously. She did not see herself as hyperactive.

Taylor gives an excellent list of the common ways hyperactive children are affected by others. He says:

It is common for hyperactive children to feel abused by others. The less the child is aware of the nature of his hyperactivity, the more unfair and malicious the criticism from others will seem to be. The child may feel as if he is always in trouble and always being blamed for something. The blaming may come from siblings, friends, teachers, parents and other family members, or even strangers.

The traits for which a hyperactive child can feel blamed are endless. Some points include being criticized for such behavior as:

—Being too noisy and making clicks, whistles, and sounds.
—Being too curious, too inquisitive, asking too many questions.
—Being too impatient, not waiting for things
—Being grabby, wanting to touch, poke, and feel things.
—Moving around the classrooms at school
—Fidgeting, drumming fingers, biting nails, chewing pencils
—Being too talkative

The child may not understand that this criticism reflects his own hyperactive behavior. He may then simply be bent on revenge.

David and I were shocked at what we read. It was if Dr. Taylor had come into our house and analyzed Stacy. She embodied every trait he described.

Taylor confirmed that the hyperactive child is often angry and fits at least partially into a troublemaker role. "They are angry with others as well as themself. Some children develop a great talent for deception." This helped us understand Stacy's ability to lie.

We welcomed the knowledge our study brought. Learning to understand our hyperactive child would benefit us as we learned to cope.

Even though I had already done some research on hyperactive children, it was an added benefit for David to agree to study with me. Even though some material was a repeat of what I had already studied, I enjoyed reading it again. I soaked up all the information on hyperactive children my time allowed.

Our study from Cantwell's book confirmed that many hyperactive traits were inherited.

Our survival kit consisted of the following tools:

(1) A knowledge gained from research.

(2) Husband/wife support that involved relieving each other from responsibilities.

(3) Providing romance and dates.

(4) Maintaining a good communication link.

(5) Participating in activities that released stress and strain.

(6) Verbal expression of appreciation.

Of all the things we were learning about surviving, romance seemed to be the most essential one. We often planned a romantic night. David loved it when I had romantic ideas. He said, "Men get tired of being the aggressors." Often, I surprised David by having a romantic evening planned at home. A candle-light dinner was inexpensive and fun. With an activity planned for the children, our evening gave us fun and quiet."

Without the fun and romance we could have easily slipped into a tragic rut. The raging storm was still there, but we had a survival that was saving our lives.

10

Saying "No" to Hate

A dictionary defines "hate" as;

1. to dislike very strongly: Cats usually hate dogs.
2. to be very averse or unwilling: I hate to travel alone
3. a strong dislike
4. an object of hatred: Snakes are her special hate.

Hate suggests strong dislike and hostility, often accompanied by a desire to hurt or harm.

The Bible says, "Love your enemies, do good to them which hate you" (Luke 6:27, KJV). The dictionary made more sense to me at that time. I had done every good thing I knew to do, and it was not good enough. In fact, Stacy's attitude was, "Aren't you going to do more for me?"

My positive attitude was more than just sour. It was gone! Resentment and hate had slowly slipped into my heart replacing my excited and determined attitude that was there when David and I were first married. I knew that feeling hate toward Stacy was wrong. I knew it was not God's way, but for the moment I did not care. I hated Stacy! I hated her for her disruptions. I hated her for the time and happiness she took away from me and David. I hated her for the terrible way she treated the other children. I hated every argument that David and I had because of a difference in opinion over Stacy. I hated the thorn in my side. I could not understand why God allowed such pain to remain. My general attitude was filled with hatefulness.

Stacy did not improve and was not learning from her mistakes. I decided something else must surely be wrong with Stacy besides being hyperactive. As a last resort we took Stacy to our family doctor again. I was clinging to a silly hope that the doctor would find something physically wrong. It seemed possible to me that she might be suffering from something we were not aware of. I was searching for answers from somewhere that might help me accept Stacy's disorder.

Stacy was never willing to admit she was hyperactive, nor would she ever consider taking her medicine regularly or going to a psychiatrist. Admitting to hyperactivity or to having psychological problems was like admitting, in her mind, that she was mentally ill. She was willing to admit that she did not understand her own actions at times, and that she did cause disruptions occasionally. Realizing these few things caused Stacy to be willing to take another series of physical tests.

Brain wave, complete blood analysis, hearing, and all kinds of tests were administered. We thought the test might reveal something somewhere that could be fixed, replaced, or taken out. We waited patiently for the result. It took one day to take all the tests, and another day for the tests to be read and studied. It was not until the third day that we went back to the doctor for the results. He announced that we had a very healthy young girl. I know my mouth must have hung wide open. The doctor noticed our obvious disappointment. He said there was not a test available to determine minor brain malfunction. He said, "Stacy's actions confirm that."

I realized I was not going to be able to move Stacy out of the house when she graduated, so I continued to investigate the other possibilities David and I had discussed after our big quarrel.

In one of our conversations, we discussed finding volunteer jobs for Stacy. The idea would be to find something simple that she could handle in a volunteer working situation and hope the volunteer job would turn into a potential paying job.

We were thrilled when we located a volunteer job at a public library. I was so excited at the potential of this job. The volunteer job would teach Stacy to report to work and follow the few instructions concerning relocating books and keeping the file system straight. I felt sure Stacy could handle a simple task like this.

A few weeks later, the librarian asked us not to bring Stacy back to the library. She explained, "Stacy talks to every person in the library. She avoids her simple task of placing books on the shelf. Instead, she gets a book, sits down with it, and reads, regardless of what I have asked her to do. She laughs and talks constantly even while she is reading!"

Those embarrassing feelings began to show on my face. I wanted to run and hide. Hate found its way back into my heart and I seemed to be overcome with discontentment. I wanted to yank Stacy up and spank her all the way to the car. Why couldn't she function in any manner at all? The librarian had at least complained in a sweet manner. I was thankful for her kind attitude.

I continued my search to find something Stacy could do. A neighbor suggested I talk to the center that assists in programs offered to handicapped children. My friend told me they were always looking for volunteer help. Many times a volunteer worker helps a child during physical therapy or runs errands or answers the phone. This seemed like a terrific idea. I immediately called and asked if Stacy might be able to do some volunteer work at this center. The director said "certainly." Once again I felt very hopeful. Stacy seemed to have a genuine love for children and surely she would be able to assist in holding an arm, or helping exercise a leg. Our hearts sank when the director called us after one week, informing us that Stacy could not come back. She explained that Stacy followed the male attendants around. She continued by telling us the manner in which Stacy flirted with every male that came into the building, whether it was a doctor or a janitor.

I could not believe it! It seemed Stacy could do nothing at all.

I was not giving up! My determination came from the fear that Stacy would be with us forever. Stacy did enjoy reading, so I laid self-help books around hoping she would pick one up and read it. As soon as she discovered it was a self-help book she tossed it down.

Several times during Stacy's senior year she actually found a job. Once she was the Easter bunny at the shopping mall during the Easter season. Her only job was to pose with children while their picture was taken. She was fired after a few days. Stacy never understood why she was dismissed. Her response was always the same, "It is their fault not mine! I have not done anything wrong!"

When we asked the manager what she had done wrong, we were told she could not sit still and that she tickled the children and playfully scared them. Also, the manager explained that on two occasions, money was missing from the cash register and she explained that Stacy had taken it. If Stacy saw someone she recognized she jumped up from her bunny seat and ran after them saying, "Guess who I really am!"

The manager's explanation sounded very familiar as I recalled the money problems we had with Stacy during the school fund-raising programs as well as the problems of sitting still.

During Christmas season, she was hired as a sales-person in a Christmas booth. She was required to maintain a small area and wait on customers. She was fired! David and I could not believe it! Stacy was not able to tell us why she was fired. We decided to ask once again. The poor frustrated owner blurted out thirty minutes of frustrations. "She simply cannot function. She sits and reads the newspaper or a book, completely ignoring customers. She flirts with every guy that passes, regardless of age." He continued, "Sometimes she leaves the booth following men, no matter what I have instructed her to do."

It was the same old complaint. It wore on our nerves like a broken record. We explained to the owner about Stacy's problems and our efforts to help. Amazingly enough, he took pity on us and agreed to give Stacy another chance. We explained to Stacy in detail what she must and must not do. We made her repeat the requirements so we could know for sure she understood. She answered our questions and seemed to understand what was expected of her. She was excited about a second chance. In a matter of days, however, she repeated the same mistakes and was fired a final time. Every idea and every avenue seemed like a dead end. Her problems grew out of control, getting larger and more complicated as she grew older.

We tried desperately to help Stacy find something that would apply to her future. Our time was running out as her senior year was coming to an end. We were an average family with an average income.

Our finances along with our emotions and nerves had been drained. At one point I thought to myself, *Maybe Stacy will fail her senior year and that will give us more time to direct her into something she could handle*.

We were so thankful the other children were growing up with minimal problems. Stacy was jealous of any talents the other children might have. Like a little child, she resented anything anyone else obtained.

We tried to do all the right Christian things. We read Scriptures and prayed. Nevertheless, the hate inside of me grew.

The verses on love and forgiveness sounded nice, but applying those truths to my own life became a real effort. It was easy to read Ephesians 3:13 "Be gentle and ready to forgive others," and Mark 11:24 "When you are praying, first forgive anyone you are holding a grudge against, so that your Father in heaven will forgive you your sins too" (TLB).

It had become so hard for me to have a loving, forgiving

nature. Not only did I have a grudge, I had hate in my heart. Rotten, stinking hate. Hate that gnaws away at your insides, and leaves you feeling sick. I always felt like hate could be compared to cancer; it slowly spreads throughout your body, destroying every living cell.

The verses on love and forgiveness were beautiful, but how was I going to apply those truths to my own life? My ugly irritating hate had spread like wildfire.

From what I understood of the Scriptures, God would not forgive me unless I forgave Stacy. It sounded easy to have a forgiving heart, but it surely was hard for me to put into practice. The more I read about forgiving others, the more I realized I had to forgive and love Stacy.

I knew what the Bible said and I believed the Bible to be God's Holy Word. I knew I had to turn loose and let God have all those ugly feelings that were causing rot and decay.

That night, I asked Stacy to join me for a talk. She did. I read her the Scriptures on forgiving and I shared the anger I felt toward her.

Stacy looked at me with an empty expression on her face. It appeared she was really surprised to hear me express my feelings of anger. I never used the word *hate*. I tried to be a little more gentle than that. I had read many times in my research that hyperactive children are not aware of their irritating habits, nor do they realize they are annoying anyone. Even though I had read this, I just could not believe Stacy was not aware of her irritating habits. We told her daily what she did that was annoying.

Seeing Stacy's expression made me realize how much she really lacked in reasoning and understanding. I had simply said, "Stacy I am sure your must know that there has been some aggravation between us. I have felt anger toward you and been disgusted with you. Please forgive me of my hateful feelings and for anything else I might have done to hurt you."

When I was finished talking, she just looked at me. I am not sure what she felt, nor could I tell if she sincerely cared how I felt. Finally she nodded her head that she forgave me, barely mumbling it aloud.

My heart pounded! I so wanted her to ask me to forgive her of the hurt she caused me. She said nothing. At last, I said, "Stacy, I forgive you of the things you have done to hurt me." She looked at me as if to say, "You mean I have hurt you?"

The conversation was short and I literally trembled with emotion. Stacy never spoke a word. It was obvious that she was limited in her comprehension and understanding. She was handicapped. Without her willingness to accept her problem, neither of us was going to get anywhere, no matter how gallant our efforts were. I had to accept and love Stacy for the handicapped person she was. She was not going to change, so I had to make changes in my attitude toward her.

11

Who *Am I* Really?

I was learning how hard it was to be honest with myself. Many expressions described my feelings, "I hate Stacy!" and "Stacy embarrasses me." There was also "I feel humiliated when Stacy acts silly and inappropriate." On and on I could go, comparing expressions with my feelings. The hard part was acknowledging I had these ugly feelings.

My talk with Stacy on forgiving forced me to face some cold hard facts. It was easy to tell her I forgave her. It was easy to ask her to forgive me; but how did I really feel? Did my actions speak louder than my words?

I conveniently put on my mask every day. A mask that covered up what I disliked about myself. Hiding my ugly feelings prevented others from knowing the "real me."

I have discovered that almost everyone wants to be liked. I wanted to be liked, too. I wanted others to admire my efforts as a stepmother. I certainly did not want anyone to see me without my mask.

Before I could truly forgive Stacy for the hurt she had caused me, I had to acknowledge my own hateful feelings. Through the years I had recognized bitterness and resentment, but my recent conversation with Stacy had only made me realize how deep my feelings ran. I was frightened at the thought of facing my own feelings and admitting to myself that I hated Stacy.

I had been hiding behind a mask for years. I had not been

in touch with myself, but now I was ready to take a good hard look at me. Who was I really?

I knew for sure that I was a Christian, desperately trying to be a nice person and follow all the teachings of the Bible. I knew I was a disappointed mother because my ideas appeared to have failed. I was continually embarrassed when a schoolteacher or adult figure of authority confronted us with some ridiculous inappropriate action of Stacy's. I felt humiliated knowing Stacy was part of our otherwise clean-cut, normal family.

Most everyone's emotions affect them. I felt like my emotions were a virus that infected my personality. I was extremely careful that the sick part of my personality did not show in public. It showed when I was alone at home.

For years I prayed the right prayers and said all the right things. Those prayers truly gave me strength, guidance, and peace. Somehow I managed to pray and still hang onto my feelings. "How can God fix the problem if I am still hanging on to it?"

With a new awareness and confession of my feelings I felt free to begin growing. I was ready to let go of those ugly feelings and let God have the problem.

I took a piece of paper and made a list of things that caused my ugly feelings to emerge. As I looked at my long list of complaints involving Stacy's behavior I realized I focused too much on my own emotional needs and not enough on hers. I felt because I was a Christian I could escape this kind of anxiety. I was not exempt! Being a Christian did however give me added strength to cope with the many problems life presented.

I wrote down all the nice things I could think of about Stacy. I gave a lot of consideration to this list. At first I could not think of any good qualities, but as I continued thinking I realized Stacy was sensitive to other people who were experiencing physical and emotional pain. She loved small animals and pets and showed attention to any need they might have. Maybe this love for animals stemmed from a rejection by her peers.

These thoughts made me recognize Stacy's ability to be sensitive and compassionate. I wrote down everything I was thankful for, which included my health and my love for David. We lived in a beautiful home and enjoyed family times together. My list of blessings grew long and I began to feel a renewing in my soul.

Then I made a list of Bible characters who had problems. I was amazed to find that most everyone, even Bible characters had problems. These characters really stood out in my mind and left an impression. My favorite was, of course, Paul with his painful thorn. The Bible never says what the thorn is but many theologians suggest the thorn to be a physical pain.

Elijah was one of God's greatest prophets but he became so depressed he wanted to die. God called Moses to deliver the Hebrews out of slavery and Moses coped with a whole group of complainers and doubters. Can you imagine how stressful his job would have been without the power of God to guide him? Job was a rich man who experienced many problems because God allowed him to be tempted. Daniel was a beloved man of God but found himself in a lions' den because he prayed. He depended on God for strength.

The list grew, and it helped me to realize that even the most beloved men of the Bible had problems. These biblical men drew their strength from heaven.

My list renewed my faith as I recommitted myself to the knowledge that God had a purpose in the pain I experienced. Because I am human I knew that I would continue to have ups and downs. The human part of me is weak and the spiritual part of me picks up the human part of me that fails.

Jesus said, "Peace I leave with you, my peace I give unto you: not as the world giveth, give I unto you. Let not your heart be troubled, neither let it be afraid" (John 14:27, KJV).

I bowed my head and began to pray what seemed to be an unending request that God might teach me through this painful experience. God already knew all about my hateful feelings. As I became truthful with myself I was at a new point in my Christian faith. I could finally see some evidence of spiritual growth. I had learned how important confession was. Confession is a major part of a Christian's growth. "If we confess our sins, he is faithful and just to forgive us our sins, and to cleanse us from all unrighteousness" (I John 1:9, KJV).

12

Viewpoints from J. J. Burianek, M.D.

It was my extreme privilege to visit with Dr. J. J. Burianek of Baytown, Texas. Dr. Burianek is a prominent pediatrician and has successfully won the love and admiration of thousands of people.

Doctors must mend, fix, overhaul, patch, rebuild, and recondition the human body. They must also express patience, love, understanding, and concern. Doctor Burianek has continually provided quality medical care as well as preserved his ability to be sensitive and compassionate toward his patients. His successful practice is proof of this high level of excellence achieved and maintained for the past twenty-six years of his medical career. He is often referred to as Dr. "B."

My interest in hyperactive children motivated me to ask Dr. "B" if I could talk with him. He graciously agreed to share his knowledge with me. He, too, had a special interest in hyperactive children.

When I made arrangements to have an interview with Dr. "B," I expected to talk with him in his office. I was pleasantly surprised when he and his wife, Sylvia, cordially invited me to their home.

My appointment day came and I anxiously drove to the proper address. The beautifully landscaped yard and circular drive was a perfect setting for their elegantly designed Southern-style home which proudly exhibited tall bold white pillars on the front porch.

"Wow," I mumbled under my breath, "this is beautiful." I rang the doorbell and Dr. "B" himself greeted me. His genuine friendliness immediately calmed my nervousness and within seconds he and his wife were talking with me. The Burianeks' down-home relaxed mannerisms demonstrated their true gift of Southern hospitality.

Dr. "B's" outstanding medical reputation is the result of hard work, determination, and parents who encouraged him throughout the struggling years. It is added support to have a good beginning and Dr. Burianek's eyes sparkled as he told with pride that he was probably one of the last home deliveries in the area.

Dr. "B" was born in the small country town of Crosby just twelve miles from his home in Baytown, Texas, where he is established and practicing today. He attended Crosby schools and, because of premedical requirements, transferred to Baytown where he attended Robert E. Lee High School.

It seemed so appropriate that he ended up where he started out. I detected a note of school loyalty when he stated his teenage girls were also attending Robert E. Lee High School.

After high school, Dr. "B" spent three years at Texas A & M and then was accepted by the University of Texas Medical Branch in Galveston where he spent four years studying for his Bachelor of Science degree and his medical degree. Dr. "B" spent one year involved in a general rotating internship in the Fort Worth area, following six months with a physician in Arlington, Texas. The Air Force engaged him in a two-year adventure that included a tour of France where he served as a base surgeon for three months. He then advanced to a larger hospital and was involved in obstetrics for nine months and then went to pediatrics. He came back to Texas to attend the Baylor medical program in Houston at Texas Children's Hospital. Dr. "B" realized at this time his real interest was in pediatrics and returned to Baytown to begin his practice.

The years of preliminary studies had been tough. His parents helped when they could, but much of the finances came from his own hard work and determination.

Dr. "B" spoke tenderly of a mother and father who continually supported and encouraged him through out the hard years of training. "I guess that is why I wanted to be closer to home, knowing how much my parents had done for me. Working hard only made me appreciate more what I have now," Dr. "B" said.

With medical credentials such as these, combined with the down-home goodness of caring, it is no surprise that Dr. "B" is such a success.

I was intrigued as he began sharing his knowledge with me concerning hyperactive children. He explained that the most popularly used term to identify hyperactive children was A.D.D. (Attention Deficit Disorder.)

"These kids cannot sit still very well and usually do not watch television for long or enjoy being read to. There is clearly an attention disorder. The hyperactive child can not concentrate which allows their hyperactivity to show up by their constant movements."

He stated that hyperactive children are smart children in most cases with high I.Q.'s. "If you can calm the child down, then he can show you how smart he really is."

Dr. "B" observed that a large number of hyperactive children are dyslexic. "When you combine hyperactivity, dyslexia, and attention disorder, you have a real problem."

Testing is important. In order to avoid labels a physician must be very careful. Testing allows the physician to know for sure if a child is hyperactive. Dr. "B" explained that a physical examination will confirm hyperactive reflexes and gross motor incoordination. If these tests confirm that the child is hyperactive, then the school is expected to assist with psychological evaluations.

"School evaluations confirm where the weak areas are. I

have found that the test results often show the hyperactive child to be weak in the areas of reading and spelling and that school assistant programs can be very helpful."

Many hyperactive children take a prescribed medication called Ritalin. I asked Dr. "B" to explain to me the usage of this drug. I learned that Ritalin was first used to combat barbiturate overdoses and that Ritalin is a stimulant. In giving a stimulant to an already stimulated hyperactive child, the drug amazingly produces an opposite reaction by suppressing the child.

"Ritalin suppresses without depressing the child." Dr. "B" explained that the child is still alert and able to learn. "Ritalin slows the problem of hyperactivity, but psychological problems already developed may need the attention of a psychiatrist."

Dr. "B" explained that different children obtain various problems.

"Psychological overlays are displayed more vividly from the disordered child when he is rejected by his own family. It is difficult for parents not to reject the disordered child because these children can be very irritating.

"Parents must learn to cope in order to help the child overcome this disorder."

Dr. "B" pointed out that the family is a unit. The child and the parent may consider psychiatric help to combat the scars resulting from a hyperactive personality disorder. "The family is a team. The whole family must learn to work with each other. If the main team member is not willing to participate, then you cannot play ball."

Dr. "B" suggested that parents:

1. Have the child evaluated
2. If appropriate, medication should be given.
3. Parents should not be frightened of the medication.

Dr. "B" stated that children who began therapy and medication at an early stage can overcome many obstacles. "I have my doubts about those who did not start out early."

It was interesting to find that many parents are concerned and frightened about a dependency on drugs if the child is given Ritalin.

"My patients who were on Ritalin as a young child are not dependent on drugs. I have been prescribing Ritalin for twenty-six years and I have not had any problems. I find that children who have been on Ritalin all of their young life look forward to the time their body no longer depends on it.

"Ritalin makes a noticeable difference and teachers are able to see the difference in hyperactive children when they are on Ritalin and when they are not. The change in their personalities are amazing.

"Children do feel an effect from the ritalin. some hyperactive children might feel a little nervous at first, but they realize they can not sit still without the medication and usually learn to overcome the effects of the Ritalin.

Some parents complain that their children suffer from a loss of appetite as a side effect to the Ritalin. "A parent must consider how a long-range chemical therapy program will affect their child's future.

"It is important not to overdo. Use only the amount of medication necessary. Parent's must become aware of the pitfalls. Basically, if your child is truly hyperactive (Attention Deficit Disorder) the purpose of the treatment is to solve just that problem so that the child can learn."

I was interested when Dr. "B" stated that many psychological problems arise from the child being hyperactive. "These problems arise because the child is different. He cannot learn in the usual way while the other kids can."

"Psychological problems must be solved through other types of therapy. Hyperactivity is solved by taking Ritalin.

"The hyperactive child must learn to accept Ritalin. Ritalin is no different than taking a heart pill or a thyroid pill or a blood pressure pill.

"Ritalin is simply a medication that will help you with a problem.

"We are a negative society," said Dr. "B." "We have conquered polio, but if we get ten cases a year from the polio vaccine then people think it is awful. In 1948, 48,000 people died from polio, and a quarter of a million were paralyzed. We have changed those statistics to ten people. We are so spoiled to the fact that we do not want to have any disease or problems. We think everything has to be perfect, but nothing is perfect. We must decide what is best and apply it.

"There is a not a lot of problems with Ritalin. Some parents and hyperactive children tend to feel that taking Ritalin is horrible, but it is not. I do not see any one having a problem if they need medication for their infection. If they need an antibiotic they do not mind asking for it. If you need Ritalin to slow down your system then you should take it."

Dr. "B's" twenty-six years of knowledge and experience was obvious from his conversation. I had only personally studied hyperactive disordered personalities for two years.

My visit with Dr. Burianek confirmed that my knowledge and understanding of hyperactive children was correct.

Dr. Burianek was one of the most pleasant individuals I had ever met. I will always admire him because of his high medical standards and his many years of experience. I will also remember that as a busy doctor he made the time for a personal visit with me.

I walked away from Dr. "B" and Sylvia's beautiful home and said to myself. "That was a very nice visit." I felt good inside as I realized many children right here in Baytown, Texas, were receiving excellent medical care from a very compassionate, loving, and understanding doctor.

13

The *Brain*

It was interesting to study the sophistication of the brain. I learned that the brain has two hemispheres and lots of specialized functions for each to control. The brain has nerve fibers, gray cells, electrical messages, and a complicated system that operates on chemical signals. The brain also depends on the aid of other systems in the body. The brain is like an automobile that must be tuned to fulfill its potential.

Doctors and scientists differ in their theories. For example, many scientists believe that some disorders, and left-handedness, stem from physical structures in the brain, but as yet no brain-behavior links have been established. Some doctors link breech birth to brain disorders. Doctors confirm that every second our brain receives countless messages from all parts of our body and the world around us. Some doctors believe that violence is often linked either to a tumor, or to some other abnormality in the brain.

Feeling sad or frightened is a normal response to crisis and fosters the strength of purpose and single-mindedness needed to cope with different levels of stress. An example would be an illness, a lost job, or a shaky marriage. The mind's perception of reality is accurate, the emotional response appropriate, and eventually, there is recovery.

Depression and anxiety are abnormal whenever they do not reflect the way things really are.

After I studied about the brain, it was easy for me to see the symptoms of a slight malfunction in Stacy's brain.

Communication takes place by dense bundles of nerve fibers called the corpus callosum. Apparently, each hemisphere has its own particular talents. In most people, the left side of the brain is good in language, mathematics, and logical thinking. Logical thinking is what Stacy lacked. The right side is important in spatial perception, musical appreciation, creativity, and intuitive thinking. Stacy lacked in intuitive thinking. If one small fraction of a malfunction occurs on either side or both sides of the brain, it causes different degrees of problems. In some cases different tests can detect brain malfunctions. All of the tests given to Stacy showed normal activity. My studies led me to believe that somewhere, somehow Stacy had minimal brain damage in some area of her brain.

I was surprised at the amount of information I located. The counselor at school recognized the possibility of minimal brain damage, and he gave us several books to read on the subject. It was an enormous help to me and very enlightening.

As a mother clinging on to every possibility, my studies gave me understanding which enabled me to cope better with Stacy.

One look at a picture of the brain reminded me of what a miracle our body is. The brain is one part of a big technical mass of systems. If everything works properly within our systems, then we are fortunate indeed.

The editor of *The Hyperactive Child*, Dennis P. Cantwell, M.D., explains that some hyperactive children may suffer from brain damage but says, "It is clear that the majority do not." Cantwell's book offered some very interesting statistics from case studies on hyperactivity. Antisocial behavior of a rather marked degree was a frequent finding.

Twenty-two percent of the children had long histories of such behavior and were considered likely to be sociopathic as adults. Nearly sixty percent had had some contact with the police and seventeen percent on three or more occasions. Nearly a quarter had been referred to the juvenile court. More than a third had threatened to kill their parents, seven percent carried weapons and fifteen percent had set fires. Two-thirds were considered by their parents to be incorrigible. The emerging picture, then, is of children who have difficulty conforming to rules, whether set by society or by their families.

Very poor school performance was also a characteristic finding.

One-quarter were attending some type of special school or class, nearly sixty percent had failed one or more grades, and nearly twenty percent two or more grades. Nearly three-quarters of the group still had concentration and attention problems in the classroom. Some sixty percent were considered by teachers to be a discipline problem, while seventeen percent had begun truanting. Finally, nearly half of the children were experiencing depressive symptoms at follow-up with frequent periods of low mood and poor self-image. Fifteen percent had either talked of or attempted suicide. Thus a significant number of these children were experiencing inner turmoil as well as having a disruptive influence on their environment.

Dr. Cantwell's findings forced us to face some scary possibilities.

14

The *Worst* Vacation Ever!

At times parents think of brilliant plans for a happier family communication. Why in the world David and I thought our family needed a time of togetherness through a vacation, I will never know.

We excitedly made plans to visit some tourist attractions within a few hundred miles of the surrounding area. We thought it would be fun to picnic, swim, sightsee, and just be close. We definitely experienced close! We were so close I thought I was going to be smothered. We packed picnic and swimming supplies, games, suitcases, and, of course, six bodies. We drove a whole ten miles before the noise started.

"How far are we going to drive today?"

"I'm hungry!"

"You can't be, we just ate before we left the house."

"I forgot to get a drink, I'm thirsty."

"I've got to go the restroom *bad!*"

On and on it went until I thought I would scream. David and I looked at each other and whispered, "Maybe this was not such a good idea after all." On the first day of our fun trip, we stopped for a picnic and made four emergency stops for restroom calls. I heard Stacy tell the others she did not really need to stop, she just wanted to ask us to buy her a snack. I realized then, that David and I were headed for the worst week of our life. We stopped driving for the day earlier than we had

planned. The children were so full of energy we could not
stand their flow of electricity any longer.

Our motel was nice and a welcome change from the car and
highway. We located our motel room, unloaded the car and
then collapsed on the bed. We had driven about seventy-five
miles in six hours. How could we have thought a vacation
with three energetic children and one hyperactive teenager
could be fun? We must have temporarily lost all of our
common sense. The children hurriedly put their swimsuits
on and ran out to play and swim. David and I continued to
lie on the bed in total shock. The quiet lasted about fifteen
minutes.

We continually heard our son say, "Stop it Stacy, stop." I
crawled out of bed and stumbled to the window. Stacy was
dunking our son and playing roughly with him by jumping on
him and splashing water in his face. I went to the swimming
pool and made Stacy come inside. I asked our son how long
Stacy had been playing so rough in the pool. I asked my
question in reference to that moment, but my son answered,
"For years!"

I was shocked. I said, "She dunks you and plays rough with
you each time you go swimming?" He answered "Yes." "Why
have you not told us?" he said, "Because Stacy told me she
would do something real bad to me." *How awful*, I thought. I
said a number of things, and emphasized the importance of
not being afraid to tell us something that upset him.

Stacy automatically became hyperactive around other people, noise, and activities. We made our corrections and kept
Stacy out of the pool the rest of the day.

The first day of our fun vacation was ending. The children
shared a room and David and I had a separate room joining
theirs. We thought the children would enjoy watching television, snacking, laughing, and being away from us. We could
hear in the next room very well so we did not fear not being
close enough. As the children watched television we heard

our youngest daughter saying, "Stop Stacy, don't sit on me anymore, I can't breathe."

David opened the door and told Stacy to stop sitting on our daughter. I called our daughter into our room and asked her if Stacy had ever sat on her like that before. She said, "All the time. She sits on top of me every time I lay on the floor to watch television. Sometimes she sits on me so long and so hard I think I am going to die."

Our vacation was allowing us to see some different problems. I could not believe she had hidden these actions toward the children from us for so long.

Stacy's psychological problems emerged through her actions toward the children as she scared them and made them believe she would hurt them. Our son trembled with fear during our conversation about Stacy dunking him. Both our daughter and son felt at times Stacy's rough playing would lead to their deaths. When you are underwater or being sat on and cannot breathe, it is very scary, especially for young children. Stacy could have very well hurt any of the children permanently.

I felt horrible that Stacy had frightened the children so badly and that we were unaware of it.

Late that night we heard Stacy complaining, "This pillow is too hard. I hate this bed. I'm uncomfortable!" Her complaints woke the others up. We then heard, "Stacy, be quiet." "No," she said, "I don't have to!" David rolled over in his bed and mumbled, "What have we done to ourselves?" He stumbled to the children's room to give out instructions and to take care of complaints.

The children complained that Stacy did nasty things. I was afraid to ask, but I did.

Occasionally, Stacy masturbated in front of the children. I was shocked to say the least! When Stacy realized this act offended the children she used it as a threat, telling the children she would finger herself if they did not do what she told them to do. I was beside myself with anger. How could Stacy be this awful when we were not around? At least our vacation revealed these awful habits and at least we were able to convince the children to come to us with their complaints. Stacy was obviously very disturbed. We were frightened as we thought of Stacy's future as well as our own.

15

My Child Is *Missing*

By the time Stacy turned eighteen, she had been employed five times and fired five times. She was engaged to be married, but that did not work out for her either and she was barely passing in school. Stacy's future looked dim.

After many hours of prayer and numerous phone calls we located a vocational school that offered a two-year program with housing available on campus.

We discussed this with her and she became very excited. She too felt a new ray of hope. After graduation from high school she could attend the vocational school away from home for two years. Our desire was that she graduate from the vocational school, find a job with the job placement program the school offered, and learn to function on an appropriate level.

I listened quietly to each member of the family and realized we all shared the same excitement. We were thrilled about the possibility of Stacy finally becoming a productive individual.

Stacy and I enjoyed shopping together as we gathered all the essentials she would need while living away from home. We were like any typical family getting ready to send a child off to college.

Everything was progressing smoothly. We were allowing Stacy extra privileges. She occupied her time in different ways. She was allowed the privilege of borrowing David's car which gave her an opportunity to make frequent trips to the public library or to our local mall. Stacy's shopping trips were unreasonably long, but we always accepted her explanation of where she had been. Knowing it was only a few months before she would be leaving for school, we tried to avoid confrontations about her behavior. Her long shopping trips meant quiet hours for us.

To our great relief, Stacy did graduate from high school. I gave her a small graduation party. I believe that she genuinely appreciated the party and the sharing of this experience. It appeared that she sincerely thought about her days of high school ending as she anticipated her future.

We made two trips to the college to establish and secure housing and other essentials. On several occasions I heard Stacy say that she could hardly wait until it was time to go. On some days I even felt that Stacy was in the process of maturing and becoming responsible. It seemed we could actually see a speck of light toward the end of the tunnel. Stacy's response and interest was a refreshing change and we enjoyed seeing more positive and less negative responses.

We were shocked when Stacy got up one morning before anyone else did and left without returning.

At first we thought she had just gone with friends somewhere and neglected to tell us, but as the day wore on and she was nowhere to be found we became worried. How far could she get without money, gas, extra clothes, or food? Where in the world could she be?

As the hours slowly passed our search became more detailed and involved. Worry grew in our stomachs. We felt sure we would find Stacy at the mall or library. After hours of searching, we realized she was either hurt or she had chose to leave on her own free will. We called the police, making her absence a legal matter. We made phone calls throughout the day and night in hopes that someone might have seen or heard from her.

By the late afternoon of the next day we were terrified with thoughts of suicide, rape, murder, or some other horrible reason for her absence. We wondered if her affectionate personality resulted in an involvement with a cruel, sick man who had viciously harmed her or killed her! We were concerned about a possible car wreck, thinking she might be hurting, or injured somewhere. A million sickening thoughts raced through our minds every minute she was gone.

The second day after Stacy disappeared, the police came to our home. They had found her. She had willingly left with a boy and had not intended to even call us. It did not even seem to faze her that we were frantic with concern. I got the feeling she enjoyed knowing we were frightened. Her attitude and responses screamed out, "I hate you!" We were confused and hurt.

She had manipulated us once again, but this time with much more ease and grace. She had cleverly manipulated us so that she could be gone for long periods of time without arousing our suspicion. She obviously had been visiting with this boy the entire summer, while telling us she was at the mall or library.

The policeman stated, "She is eighteen which makes her a legal adult. She has not broken any laws and we cannot legally make her come home." I blurted out in anger, "What about the car she stole?"

"Do you want to press charges," I heard the officer say. for an instant I was silent. In that one instant a million things went through my mind. She was so ungrateful. Would we lose the money we had invested toward her tuition? What would we do without David's work car? David and I looked at each other and then decided we would not press charges.

I fought my nagging hateful feelings. I wanted her to *pay* for the worry she had caused. I wanted her to suffer for treating us so hatefully. I was so outraged with anger that I felt like literally beating Stacy to a pulp.

Sensing the extent of our broken hearts and the pain we felt, the policeman gently spoke, "I've seen thousands of cases just like this one. For some reason the child rebels against everything they have been taught. Kids like Stacy are given every opportunity in the world and they still rebel. Parents and other members of the family sacrifice continually for this one child." He continued, "She has made her choice now let her live with it. It is time for your family to continue living without the emotional strain that Stacy presents.

"Some children," he said, "learn while others grow up to be adults, never changing or learning. They continually burden their families. They go through life convincing others to provide for them. Let her go.

"It will be hard to make a stand but you must, before she destroys your whole family," the officer said.

The policeman had given us excellent advice. Even though it would be hard, we would allow Stacy the privilege of living with the decision she made. With the policeman's encouragement, Stacy called home that night.

David had a long talk with her about the many things she should consider. He encouraged her to come home and continue plans for the vocational school. She insisted she did not want to come back, not now, not ever. David reminded her of the consequences of her decision. He explained to her several times that she would not be allowed to move in and out of the house but that she had this one last opportunity to come home. She was told there would be no more disruptions nor would we rescue her when she got in trouble. "The game of life is not an easy one to play and you must learn to follow the rules," he said. He confronted her about stealing the car. Her response was that of continual unconcern.

Parents often go the extra mile and in many cases an extra hundred miles. David realized Stacy had made up her mind. He had a need to give her a good start, just like many parents would want to do. He transferred the car's title, giving her legal ownership. He drew our out small savings of several hundred dollars and gave it to her. When she came to the house to pick up her belongings, she realized how many nice things she had. Packing and moving took a little longer than she had anticipated. She had forgotten about her stereo, bowling ball, collection of pretty ceramics, and other beautiful possessions.

Stacy acted as if her life with us had been miserable but, in time, she would learn how comfortable we had made her life.

She lacked training for any possible career and only had the shallow promise of a boy she had known a few weeks.

Recognizing she was mentally unbalanced as well as hyperactive, I knew we would not be able to turn her away if she came back. As I recognized this, I also recognized that our family could not tolerate Stacy's disruptions any longer. We knew we could not allow Stacy to stay with us if we were to remain mentally stable and have any peace and happiness at all. Feeling these emotions, I began to call the many agencies that assist young adults with similar disorders. I was surprised at the long list of possibilities.

I was absolutely positive that it would only be a matter of time before Stacy returned. When she did return, I would refer to one of these agencies and together we would think of the best possible answer for her and the family.

My haunting, hateful feelings returned and I found myself thinking of ways I could get even. I wanted her to be miserable the way she had made me.

I continually looked toward heaven when these hateful feelings emerged and said, "I haven't learned yet have I, God?"

16

Mending the Family

As time passed, we were amazed at Stacy's ability to persuade others to take care of her. She lived with one man and then another: her only interest seemed to be for someone to provide for her physical needs and material desires. Stacy's overly affectionate nature was seemingly going to make her life fairly simple. She formed a pattern quickly of living with men who were willing to take care of her. When one grew weary of her disordered personality and asked her to leave, she simply moved in with another.

I was shocked that Stacy never asked to come back home. When things got a little difficult for her, she just moved.

With someone else taking the financial burden off her shoulders, it seemed she was having the time of her life. No rules, no parents, no finances, and no problems.

She never picked up the phone to call. Months went by without our hearing from her or knowing where or with whom she was living. Stacy did pop in one day and proudly announce a future marriage. She acted as if we were to drop everything and join her at the courthouse for the casual exchange of wedding vows which would take place the following day. We were first amazed at the invitation, and then we were amazed at her expecting us to be there. She had not considered our feelings for months. She had not even let us know where she was. Now, given a day's notice, we were expected to shower her with our blessings.

It was not possible for us to attend the ceremony and, as usual, when Stacy did not get her way she became angry. She showed her anger in a vindictive way by telling others she had been physically abused and kicked out of the house. She again reminded everyone that we were not her real parents. I am not sure if that was to make her accusations more believable or if it was her way of continually disowning us.

She made a concentrated effort to tell people she came in contact with that we did not love her or care about her. I was amazed at her ability to lie and then to believe her own lies. She had convinced herself that these things were true. Once again our pain penetrated to the bone.

Our family slowly began feeling the relief of Stacy's absence. We felt we had been the victims of a terrible fire and were left with open wounds from the burns. It would take months to heal. Just as one might feel physical pain, our emotions caused severe discomfort. The soothing lotion for our wounds was the peace and quiet we were experiencing. The absence of Stacy and her many disruptions was like a relaxing day on a sunny beach. We soaked up her absence the way one might soak up the sun. We felt a wonderful peace that we had never felt before.

No longer did we experience the daily explosions over bathing, shampooing, using soap, shaving underarms, using deodorant, or brushing teeth. She was gone.

Within a few months we began planning vacations and simple outings to the beach or lake. Stacy's absence made a remarkable difference.

The longer Stacy was gone the more we felt the healing process taking place. I realized the impact of Stacy's problem had truly taken me away from the other children. I felt sorry that our kids had been forced to face the potency of Stacy.

Our experiences had been a trial that lasted for many painful years. The hardest part was behind us and the healing part was in progress.

We began to focus on the other children and apply new efforts to help each child deal with the emotional damage that had been caused from our raging storm. Time seemed to be the key factor. In time, we would all recover from our emotional trauma.

We made a concentrated effort to direct our children into an activity that focused on special talents. These talents would improve their self-esteem. We praised them for each accomplishment. We went to their recitals, rehearsals, and sporting events. We supported the activities our children played in, sang for, danced to, or acted in. We were there to watch and praise them for their performances.

We created a family time in which we all gathered to talk about our deepest thoughts. No matter how ugly those feelings were it was important to share them. Expressing those feelings among our family comforted each of us as we realized our feelings we not so different after all.

Some children needed more individualized attention. Art therapy and counseling contributed to the success of mending torn emotions. Family activities molded a special togetherness that comforted. Picnics, trips to nearby attractions, football games, and other activities were helpful. We were all learning what it was like to be a family without disruptions.

A very memorable family event was an annual talent show which gave each of us an opportunity to display our talents in front of our small family audience.

In years to come this simple form of family entertainment would provide confidence to perform in front of school and church audiences. Our talent show was fun, entertaining, and healing.

Stacy had been married a few months when she asked for financial help.

We remembered the advice given by the policeman. "Do not allow her to destroy your entire family. Take a stand." I benefited by reading *Tough Love* by Phyllis and David York and Ted Wachtel. One comment made in that book really stuck with me. It said. "The customary method of problem solving, reasoning, scolding, punishing, and counseling have not worked. The destructive behavior usually resumes and is more severe. The act of taking a stand removes the ability of destructive young people to generate crises for others and puts that power in the hands of parents."

It was up to us to stop Stacy from generating crises in our family. It was unfair that five suffer because of one. Even in realizing this, it took us time to take our stand. We paid several bills for Stacy and her husband. We bought groceries once and gave them a number of things to help maintain their home. I was disappointed she did not express any appreciation. The more we gave the more they wanted and the more they expected.

After a few of these disappointing episodes, we realized we must take a stand or be drained financially the rest of our lives. We began saying no to the request for money and "things." Quickly they stopped asking us and began asking others who would give.

They were able to obtain some jobs, but within weeks the jobs were lost because of their inability to follow the rules. Mistakes were made and repeated and repeated and repeated.

I enjoyed watching the movie, *Karate Kid.* An Oriental man named Mr. Miyagi was very gifted in karate. His young friend named Daniel became a student in which he would teach confidence, patience, and the art of performing karate.

Oriental people seem generally gifted with wisdom and traditionally pass down this knowledge obtained to the next generation. Mr. Miyagi shared stories with Daniel that offered great truths concerning life. At one point in the movie Mr. Miyagi demonstrated how to achieve a difficult task by finding a balance. He taught Daniel the importance of balance in accomplishing any chore.

As Daniel encountered a friendship with a young girl who came from an affluent family, Mr. Miyagi warned, "Look for the balance Daniel, look for the balance."

He taught Daniel the importance of balance in accomplishing any chore. "Not too much and not too little," Mr. Miyagi would say.

We seek a balance in our lives as we strive to maintain stability.

Balance became a word that I focused on. "Not too much and not too little." If I could find the balance in my life, I could be in harmony with those around me. I realized my life was like a song. I could either be in tune or out of tune. Having a balance would make all the difference in how my song sounded.

When the Christmas season approached, we looked for the balance as we planned an early Christmas celebration with Stacy and her husband. Stacy's in-laws allowed them the privilege of staying in a family-owned apartment and we made plans to fellowship with them at their apartment. This would eliminate the strain the children might feel in her presence. We did not force any child to participate in the celebration and only one child chose to come with us for the visit.

This occasion was very difficult for David and me. We wanted to have some type of celebration with Stacy and out of obligation we felt it was our duty as parents to find a balance at Christmastime. These feelings were our only justification for putting forth an effort. We were nervous and tense as we prepared for our visit. Recognizing my own stress as an adult I could not expect our children to participate in an activity that was causing me, the adult, so much stress.

I had searched for just the right gifts to give to Stacy and her husband. We arrived at our appointed time. Stacy had cleaned the living area and hung sheets over the door openings leading into the other rooms.

I tried to create a happy conversation, but the expressions

on each face made it very clear that we all felt strained. Stacy offered us tea to drink. She seemed nervous as she prepared the tea for us. We thanked her when she handed us the tea glasses.

I brought four gifts for Stacy and four gifts for her husband, along with some special, beautiful handmade decorations. I opened the large sack holding the gifts. We watched Stacy and her husband open each gift. They never expressed any thanks or appreciation. Their facial expressions were cold as they mumbled a few words like "I needed these," or "I can use this." We sat very still and felt sad at the response we received. Stacy said, "I have a Christmas card for you somewhere." She looked but was not able to find it. I recognized the panic in her actions when she was unable to find the card.

We thanked Stacy and her husband for letting us come. We hugged them, wished them a merry Christmas, and told them we loved them.

When we got in the car Stacy came running to us saying, "I found the card." We took it and thanked them again. As we drove home, I opened the card. It said "Merry Christmas to all of you." By the time we got home my frustration showed in my voice and actions. Finally I started crying.

I was glad we had an early Christmas celebration with Stacy. Our frustrations and tension that emerged in Stacy's presence would have ruined our Christmas celebration with the others. As the days went by, we were able to compose our nerves and enjoy the festivities of the holiday season by celebrating with our children still living at home.

We had found the balance by celebrating with Stacy and having a separate celebration with the others.

Months rolled by and we continued to do polite things. The feelings remained the same and our times with Stacy only caused stress for all of us.

Even though Stacy was married, she typically was unable to function as a housewife. The apartment stayed unmanageable as did her life. It was only a mater of time before they obtained credit cards. I was amazed that they were even able to qualify for them. A credit card can be a terrible temptation for anyone. Before long, creditors were calling, cards were canceled, and a bad credit rating was established.

These were the "rules" David was talking about when Stacy first left home. I wondered if she had even given a second thought to that conversation.

Stacy and her husband abused the privileges of the free apartment. The lack of concern for cleanliness and routine care caused serious problems.

Arguments between the couple and the in-laws were frequent. Then the arguing became too frequent and too loud, Stacy decided to leave. Without warning she just got up one day and left, just as she had done when she was eighteen.

Her husband was devastated and felt sure something awful had happened to her. We certainly could identify with the heartbreaking feeling of hopelessness. We did not fear any terrifying problem, though, because of our previous experiences. Stacy's husband was frantic with worry. The police found evidence that led them to believe Stacy had left willingly with a truck driver headed across the country. We were not surprised that Stacy left with another man. She was easily persuaded and her overly affectionate personality surely enticed men. Finding her became an impossible task. Her husband tried many times to locate Stacy and finally received enough information to accept that she left willingly.

I felt sorry for him and his parents. They had tried so hard. It was difficult for them to understand that Stacy left because she wanted to. Understanding why Stacy did the things she did was always the hardest part, because, as a general rule, there was not any reason behind her actions.

Four months went by and out of the clear blue Stacy called. She wanted to come back to her husband. We were surprised that her husband wanted her back, knowing she had been with a truck driver for so many months. Once again the in-laws gave them permission to stay in the family-owned apartment. The in-laws established rules stating they must respect the rights of others and their privacy and, in general, the rules stated that they must function on an acceptable adult level and become responsible young people by maintaining a job and paying their bills.

A new family influenced Stacy's life now. They, too, would experience disappointments before they could accept Stacy's disorder. Quarreling and problems erupted once again. The in-laws continued giving and sacrificing their own happiness. Stacy and her husband were not able to follow the rules.

We could not and would not suffer any longer for one person's inability to function. The in-laws had the same privilege to say no, but they chose not to. They continued to hope things would change, and that eventually both Stacy and her husband would learn to follow simple rules.

We continually looked for the balance. We searched for ways to have a friendly relationship and yet carefully protect the emotions of our children and ourselves. We refused to feel guilty. The tough love approach was saving our sanity.

I do not know why life is like it is. I do not know why some are strong and some are weak. I do not know why some inherit good genetic chemistries and others do not. I do not know or understand why some are born with different degrees of brain damage.

I do know that God is love and that He loves all of us no matter what our problems are. I do know there is no circumstance that God will not supply extra strength to endure. I do know that God cares and that it is better to keep my eyes on Him instead of panicking. I do know His permissive will can strengthen my character. I do know that I will trust Him; although I may not understand.

Six months had gone by when Stacy became pregnant and had a baby. David went to be with Stacy in the hospital after the baby came. I was unable to go because of activities with the other children. I am sure I used that as an excuse. However, I did write her a note telling her how happy I was for her. When she came home from the hospital with the new baby, we visited several times at her apartment. We provided a cradle, a baby swing, a few infant clothes, and disposable diapers. We took pictures and tried to be the happy grandparents we were supposed to be. We could not help but feel that Stacy was not able to properly take care of a baby.

Stacy seemed to love the baby deeply, but that did not change her bad habits or her inabilities to follow simple rules. She expected more and more to be given to her after the baby came.

We still maintained our firm stand by keeping a friendly but cautious relationship. We gave when we could give. Eventually, fussing occurred between the in-laws. Stacy, husband, and baby left with some friends after a bad quarrel.

We became aware of this situation only through a phone call from the in-laws. We were aware of Stacy's traits and we were sad she had not outgrown any of them. The in-laws were concerned about the baby and could only hope that Stacy would take care of it.

Stacy never called us to say good-bye or to inform us of their move. We had put forth a sincere effort to be kind. Our efforts, gifts, friendliness, and financial assistance had not even been acknowledged. It was if we had done nothing. *What have we done so bad that Stacy does not have a desire to even talk to us?* I thought.

A phone call from the in-laws informed us of a return visit Stacy made in order to leave the baby. Then Stacy returned to her husband. We did not offer any assistance in raising the baby. It was Stacy's responsibility, not the in-laws, not ours, but Stacy's. The in-laws were angry toward us for not helping with the baby. We felt their anger should have been directed at Stacy.

17

Who Will Pay the *Consequences?*

Stacy forced me to recognize my own weaknesses. Without the pain or problems Stacy created I would not have leaned so heavily upon the Lord. I had so many ups and downs in my spiritual growth, I often though of myself suffering from the 'Yo-yo" syndrome! I know how to pray and what to say, but following through became a different story.

I knew according to the Bible I was supposed to love even my enemies. I released my hate to God sometimes, and then other times I felt like my hate resembled a forest fire burning wildly out of control.

Why was I still struggling with my feelings? I knew what was right and what was wrong. Why couldn't I consistently allow God to control my hateful feelings?

I might not have so readily referred to Bible stores if it had not been for the pain I felt as I tried to cope with Stacy. I have already mentioned the Bible character, Paul, and how through the years I had turned to the Scriptures for comfort many times. Reading about Paul gave me extra strength. He seemed to have as many problems as I did. Paul did not always handle each problem with dignity either! Paul says in Romans 7:19-20 "When I want to do good I don't; and when I try not to do wrong, I do it anyway. Now if I am doing what I don't want to, it is plain where the trouble is: sin still has me in its evil grasp" (TLB).

I could identify with these feelings. I knew different ways I could reach out to Stacy to show her my love, but the hate brewing inside of me lingered and I did not reach out. At times I felt like I had everything under control and that I had completely given my anxieties to God. In this spirit I planned some nice activity like the Christmas celebration to express my Christian love. Being around Stacy only brought out my ugliness. I felt like I continually took one step forward and two steps back!

I knew the hate that lingered in my heart was a sin. I had not yet learned to release my hate totally to God. Only in time and through God's love would I learn to allow the Holy Spirit to have full control of my thoughts and actions.

My pastor has often said that rejection is the most painful experience an individual can endure. I agree. I felt rejected by Stacy. I felt I had failed. I did not know what I could have done differently but it was obvious that I had failed somewhere.

My wonderful ideas and good intentions had not worked. With Stacy gone I had no feelings of obligation to contact her and try to talk with her. She must have had some festering wounds herself not to even call! Stacy was gone and I was glad. I could not bring myself to call her. I was glad she did not feel the need to call us.

Occasionally, throughout the year, we heard progress reports from Stacy's in-laws. Even the mention of Stacy's name caused me to cringe. I was not interested in her life or activities. It seemed like the same old repeated story to me. She and her husband had jobs. They lost jobs. They did not pay their bills and they found friends to take care of them no matter where they were located. Hearing about their problems was such a repeat of previous problems that it just made me feel worse to be made aware of them.

One day David and I went shopping together and as we stood in the checkout line with our merchandise, we were surprised to hear a voice say "Hello!" We turned our heads to see Stacy's mother-in-law standing in the checkout line next to ours. Instantly, I was nervous and tense.

David and I both said hello in a pleasant voice. The mother-in-law began telling us all of the latest news concerning Stacy and her husband. She announced that they were still living out of state and had been employed several times. The shocking news came when she said, "Stacy is pregnant again." As the mother-in-law spoke she held Stacy's first child. I wondered how Stacy was going to take care of a new baby when she was not able to raise the one she had.

The checkout line moved and before we knew it our conversation was over. When we got in the car I actually felt nauseated. My hateful feelings had made me sick to my stomach. I continued thinking about Stacy and another child to be born into their lives. How would they care for this child?

I occasionally visited with a friend who was raising a grandchild. Even though they loved the child, they were constantly worn out physically.

They were frustrated at their grown adult child for not feeling any responsibility toward the baby. The grandparents were saddled with a tremendous responsibility and allowed their children to cheat them out of their golden years.

After having the experience of raising a big family, I am anxious for the time the children will be grown and responsible for themselves. Enjoying my later years with David without the stress of raising children sounds wonderful to me. I can not imagine starting over again with a brand-new baby.

Having a family and raising children is a blessing from God. Raising children is the hardest challenge any parent can experience. I know there are exceptions to every rule, but unless emergency circumstances prevent it, I will not raise a grandchild. I deserve my golden years. I have earned the right to enjoy my grandchildren without raising them. Growing older has made me realize I don't have the same energy I had when I was younger.

There are thousands of young married couples on a long waiting list who want to adopt a baby. These couples long for the opportunity to raise a family. I have already experienced the joy as well as the pain of being a parent. Why is it so wrong that I influence my adult child who had an unplanned baby to make a decision toward the future of that child? If I agree to raise their child, I have relieved them of tremendous responsibility, and cheated myself. Children always seem to know just what to say to make parents feel guilty.

Why doesn't the adult child feel guilty? What is the difference if the baby is given to Grandma or to a young energetic couple longing to have a baby? The difference is that the adult child has manipulated an arrangement that he can live with in good conscience. It does not sound so bad if they can see their unplanned child occasionally and this is a comfort which gives them a better feeling about themselves.

I had mixed emotions toward Stacy's mother-in-law. By taking on the responsibility of raising Stacy's baby she cheated Stacy and her son out of a growing experience.

Stacy had an obligation to either be a mother or place her baby in the hands of young, fresh adults longing to be parents. The mother-in-law was not under any obligations. The obligation was Stacy's and her husband's.

I questioned in my mind who would raise the second child. How much responsibility was the mother-in-law willing to relieve the adult children of? The mother-in-law was suffering the consequences of her grown child's choices.

18

Unconditional *Love*

Stacy turned twenty while she was pregnant with her second child. Her life had made many changes during the previous two years. Now she lived in a completely different environment. I wondered if Stacy ever missed the nice things she had while she lived at home.

I had spent those two years recovering from the damage caused by Stacy's disordered personality. I enjoyed every minute of the peace and quiet I experienced during her absence.

I was puzzled at Stacy's display of bitterness. Why didn't she have a desire to call us? I was angry with her for not appreciating us and also for talking badly about us, but I did not really consider that there may be a reason why she had not called.

Stacy's silence was really a message. The message said, "You don't really like me. Your lack of understanding had made me feel that you really don't care about me." I had tried in many ways to express my love and concern for Stacy. She obviously did not feel my actions were sincere, and I guess they really were not.

Maybe when I tried to help Stacy improve her appearance she interpreted my actions as not accepting her the way she was.

In fact, my interpretation of Stacy was unacceptable and surely Stacy felt those negative feelings from me.

During the past two years I was so busy healing from my own hurt, I hadn't stopped to think about Stacy's hurt. I was so filled with anger, bitterness, and hate that I did not care why Stacy did not call us or share any part of her life with us. It took two years of being absent from Stacy for me to even consider that Stacy might be just as hurt as I was. In my reconditioned state of mind I was able to stop and consider Stacy's side of the story.

I had tried everything I knew to try, but Stacy could still feel that I did not accept her. She had severe psychological problems and an extremely disordered hyperactive personality. She did not choose this personality; it was given to her free of charge, unasked for, and unwanted.

Her disordered personality was not capable of understanding.

I had formulated many ideas in an attempt to help improve Stacy's character, but I had never accepted her or totally understood her problems. I had spent hours researching hyperactive children so that I could understand Stacy better, but how could I fully understand her problem unless I could live inside of her disordered hyperactive body for a while?

Tim LaHaye is the author of *Your Temperament Can Be Changed*. The first chapter of that book is titled "You're Born with It !"

Stacy could not help that she was disordered but I had never accepted that fact. Circumstances had sadly influenced her choice and those choices had affected her entire life.

The tugging feeling in my heart and the little voice inside of me was the Holy Spirit.

John 10:10 says. "I am come that [you] might have life, and that [you] might have it more abundantly" (KJV). This abundant life is only possible as we are filled with the Holy Spirit. I was learning that being Spirit filled was mine for the asking and that the asking should come every day and all during the day.

"Dear Lord," I prayed, "I know you have heard these words time and time again.

"All these years I have prayed the right prayer, but I never truly let go. I thought I did let go many times but I did not. thank you for never leaving me during this trial. Thank you for carrying me when I could not walk."

David and I had been married seven years when I realized, once again, I was trying to fix things my way instead of allowing God to fix things His way.

Different situations occurred to reinforce my thoughts.

One Sunday my pastor preached a sermon on unconditional love. He basically said that in our own strength we cannot love the unlovable. Only through the power of the Holy Spirit can we allow God's love to flow through us.

It was one thing to say it the right way, but another thing to do it the right way. God's love knows no exceptions. He loves Stacy the same as He loves me and just as much as He loves me. He never excludes anyone, but I had excluded Stacy. The thorn in my side had remained for such a long time because I had not learned the lessons God wanted me to learn. It was very clear to me that the lessons I must learn were acceptance, patience, and unconditional love.

During the next month I was reminded through songs, sermons, and other illustrations that I could only learn to love unconditionally if I was filled with the Holy Spirit.

For years I felt like I truly loved Stacy. Now I realized I had only been going through the motions and, even though Stacy was disordered, she could feel the difference.

"Lord, forgive me," I prayed. "Teach me how to allow your Holy Spirit to control me." Galatians 5:22-23 says, "The fruit of the Spirit is love, joy, peace, longsuffering, gentleness, goodness, faith, Meekness, temperance" (KJV). "But the greatest of these is love" (I Cor. 13:13, NASB). I wanted to obtain the greatest gift, the gift of love.

Psychologists and psychiatrists agree that the basic needs of people are love, understanding and acceptance.

Many times I asked myself after some wonderful idea had

fallen short of my expectations where I had failed. I realized I had failed in Stacy's basic needs of love, understanding, and acceptance.

I prayed, "Lord, is it too late? can I maintain a balance, demonstrate tough love as a means of teaching, and also have unconditional love? Can I be sensitive to the emotional needs of all those who still live in this house and still love Stacy? Teach me, Lord. Show me."

The Lord immediately began to show me through books, articles, and people.

I have already mentioned Tim LaHaye. I admired this author because of his books on temperance. I never dreamed the Lord would open the door and arrange for me to meet this nationally famous author. Dr. LaHaye serves at Prestonwood Baptist Church in Dallas, Texas. His family enrichment class is transmitted live via satellite to many churches each Sunday.

My mother lives in a small town near Dallas, and on one of my visits with her we decided to visit Prestonwood Baptist Church. We attended Dr. LaHaye's class on family enrichment.

It was a thrill for me to see Tim LaHaye in person. It was an added joy to attend his class. I scribbled down notes on his wonderful lesson about the family and faith.

He started out by saying, "Faith can keep the dream alive in your heart." That open statement certainly got my attention. His lesson of faith discussed the preparations Christians should make to be used of God. Some of the key points of his lesson were these:

1. Visualize by faith your goals and write them down, and stay positive.

2. Anticipate the superabundant life God has in store for you.

3. Ask God specifically what you want.

4. God is merciful.

5. Seek first the kingdom of God.

6. In everything give thanks.

This was another occasion that I would treasure forever. I would never forget this day. I thanked the Lord for continually confirming His message to me through inspirational people like Tim LaHaye.

I had brought two of his bestselling books with me. One was titled *Spirit Controlled Temperament*, and the other was *Anger Is a Choice*. He smiled, autographed the books, talked to me for a few brief moments, and gladly posed for a picture. I have the memories of this day safely tucked away in my heart.

19

A Letter to *Stacy*

Because I had a better attitude, I was able to feel the guidance of the Holy Spirit. Every spiritual lesson I had learned was put to the test sooner than I had expected. One evening David picked up the newspaper and, as usual, began reading every word on every page. Suddenly he put down the paper and looked at me strangely. I said, "What is the matter, honey?" He explained that he had just read the birth announcements and among them was that of Stacy's new baby. He continued by saying that our names were printed in the paper as grandparents and that the baby was born in a local hospital.

We could not believe she had come back to this area to give birth to her second baby. Did they live here now? How could she have put the announcement in the paper and avoided telling us? How long had she been in this area? We thought Stacy and her husband lived out of state. Was this another silent message? What did the message say?

After a few days, David came home from work and told me he had talked to his aunt. His aunt told David she had talked to Stacy while shopping one day. Stacy informed the aunt that we did not love her or care about her and that we would not even talk to her.

My spiritual thoughts pounded away at my conscience. I wanted to call, but how could I when this information made me so angry? How could she have said those things? It was she who would not talk to us. I wanted to make peace and love her unconditionally, but didn't Stacy have to love me, too? Did I have to love her without her loving me?

I fought my nagging, hateful feelings and began to pray for the Holy Spirit to fill me with love. I prayed for guidance, and then came the idea of a letter. A letter would allow me to share everything I wanted to share without interruptions. Stacy most likely would read a letter out of curiosity, whereas she might not listen to what I would say. A letter would be a message in writing that she could reread over and over again. So I made up my mind to write and send a letter to Stacy.

"Dear Stacy,

"I'm sure this letter will come as quite a shock to you. I have felt the need to write to you for a long time. I have hesitated to write or call because you interpret my statements differently than how I mean them. It seems we can say something and the next time we hear it, it is not at all what we said. Anyway, I wanted to write and I hope nothing I say is taken the wrong way.

"Now that you are the mother of two children, maybe you can realized how hard being a parent is. If a mother has the total responsibility and total care and financial burden, then she has some hard work. I am not sure how much responsibility you have. It appears from what few things we have seen that your mother-in-law has most of the responsibility instead of you and your husband. In that case you may never realize the full stress parents feel during the time they raise their children.

"Your daddy is not perfect, neither am I. We all make mistakes and do things that others disagree with. It is only natural that your opinions and our opinions are different. Can you imagine the pain you might feel if one of your children decided to never talk to you again because his or her opinions were different?

"The first Christmas you were gone from home, we hoped you would call. We left the gifts we had for you under the tree a week after Christmas was over. You never did call or come by. I stored the gifts in the closet. We made a special effort to celebrate Christmas with you last year. I thought we had a good visit. I brought over gifts and decorations. I am sure you do not remember this, but you never even said thank you until I asked you if you liked the things we brought. After Christmas you came over a few times to visit and I thought the visits were nice. Because we have three children and we are involved in so many activities from school and church we did ask you to call first. I thought I asked you nicely, but I guess you interpreted that statement as us not wanting you to come over. After that statement, you stopped coming.

"When you had your first baby, Daddy came to the hospital to see you. We gave you a baby cradle, swing, infant clothes, and disposable diapers. We came to your apartment several times to see the baby.

"We were deeply hurt when you took the baby and you and your husband left out of state for employment.

"You did not call when you left. You never called at all. You were in this area for a day when you brought your baby to your mother-in-law for her to take care of. It only takes a few minutes to call but you did not call even then. After a short length of time you and your husband came back to this area seeking different employment, but again you did not call.

"The plain truth is, you are uncomfortable around us and we are uncomfortable around you. You misinterpreted our efforts to correct and guide you as mean and hateful. You can only remember the things that upset you and made you mad. The situations you did not like were so strong on your mind, it shadowed out all of the good situations. You left without even a good-bye or thank you. You took your daddy's work car with no intentions of ever returning it. You acted very inappreciative towards the money Daddy gave to you, and the title to

the car. You cut off ties with us, but somehow have convinced
yourself that it is we who have disowned you. We heard from
one of your school friends that you told everyone we kicked
you out of the house and that we were mean to you and
physically abused you. The hurt came to us again when we
realized you believed those things. You have convinced yourself that this is what happened.

"You do not remember the nice home we provided for you
that was warm in the winter and cool in the summer. You
certainly never went hungry and you had clothes in such
quantity that it took you several trips to get them all. You
were surprised at how much you had to pack when you
decided to leave home. Your beautiful stereo, collections of
records and albums, bowling ball, skates, beautiful jewelry,
colognes, and other nice things took up more room in your car
than you thought it would. Will you be able to provide these
nice things for your children?

"We allowed you to be in the high school band and participate in band trips. Those trips cost money. That form of
entertainment and fun was not free. You were also in
R.O.T.C. and made trips with them. You went skating almost
every week when it was not football season and you were not
watching the high school football game.

"You had several boyfriends and we always made them feel
welcome. Do you remember when your boyfriends shared
Thanksgiving and Christmas dinner with us? Do you remember how I always got them very nice Christmas gifts just to
please you and show them that we cared?

"I remember giving one of your boyfriends a little graduation party. These occasions were not free. It costs money to
buy gifts and have parties.

"You always had extremely nice Christmases and birthdays.
I went to a lot of trouble to surprise you with special gifts. On
two occasions you needed a formal for a school function. We
got you the formal of your choice.

"Remember the times we went out to eat together as a family? Eating out is expensive but we managed to provide that form of fun.

"There were many times I took you to the beauty shop for hair styling or haircuts. Remember the homecoming mums I got for you? That was just because I loved you, no other reason. Remember the summers at the YMCA swimming? That was not free. We had to buy a summer membership in order to participate in the activities the YMCA provided. Do you remember the appreciation day I created just for you? We wanted you to feel loved and appreciated so I gave you a party with a cake and presents for no other reason than to show you our love. I am glad I have pictures of all this. Since you cannot remember, I can show you.

"We had all of these fun family activities and you can only remember the bad. You rebelled over anything we did to help guide you. You interpreted any kind of correction or guidance as mean and unjustified. It has always seemed to me that you felt like others should quickly forgive and forget about your mistakes, but you do not know how to forgive others when you feel they have hurt you.

"I only had you five years. I tried everything I could try to help you. But you were too mad at your daddy for marrying me and too mad at your adopted mother for dying and too mad at your biological mother for giving you away.

"Let's look at your mistakes for a minute, the men you lived with before you married, and the truck driver you ran off with for four months! How would you have felt if your husband had not been forgiving towards you?

"Do you remember the time I sat you down at the kitchen table and asked you to forgive me of the things I had done to hurt you? You were a senior. I doubt you remember. You do not seem to remember anything nice we ever did for you, but we had that talk. You said you forgave me of the things I had done to hurt you, but you never asked me to forgive you for things you did to hurt me. In your mind you had not done anything to hurt me, but let me assure you, you have done many, many things to hurt me. In your mind we were wicked people who beat you, never allowed you to go anywhere or to do anything. In general, we were just hateful all the time toward you. We know that is how you felt (and still feel) because of the many statements people have repeated to us that you made. You had a wonderful life; you just couldn't see it. You were too occupied with being mad at everyone. You walked out on your good life without even a good-bye. You have told everyone how we cut you off and disowned you. Stacy, you have disowned us! I have seen your daddy cry because of your coldness and the lies you are telling and believing yourself.

"We can never do for you what your mother-in-law does for you. We are not willing to continue to raise children when they become adults. It is beyond my wildest imagination how you and your husband can take advantage of your mother-in-law the way you do. She provides your living. We are not willing to do that!

"We can all make excuses about why this happened and why that happened. We all have problems. As adults we have to face our responsibilities and cope with our problems, not run from them!

"Daddy and I have lived our lives of heartaches and troubles, stress, and strain. Our problems are more than enough. We do not care to take on yours, too! Do you think it is right for a grown child to cheat her parents out of their golden years? I don't. I cannot even imagine you and your husband cheating your in-laws the way you are cheating them. We simply will not ever allow that kind of behavior from our grown children. The choice is ours, and we do not choose to be abused by grown children. We told you many times that when you became an adult you would be responsible for yourself.

"I hoped that some day you would show signs of maturing. I did not think you would always depend on another adult to take care of you and your children. Someday your children might ask you why you depended on others to raise them.

"Life is hard. All of us would like to blame someone or something because of our unfortunate circumstances. Our inabilities are only what we allow them to be. There are many happy stories about children who survived tragic circumstances and rose above the situation to learn from it and become better adults because of their circumstances. Then there are others who let their past keep them from growing. They live only to blame others for their mistakes and misery.

"Even though you left without a good-bye we continued to try to keep harmony with you. We gave your husband tools, a bicycle, paid your rent twice, bought Christmas gifts and gifts for the baby. We gave you birthday money, and signed a loan note at the bank so that you might purchase a car. It is too bad you gave away the car Daddy provided for you. I never understood why you stopped paying on the loan. I know many times you had money, but just did not pay the bank note because you knew we would have to. You could have at least called and apologized for not paying it. This is another example of the way you treat others.

"If someone does not treat you right, or you do not think they are treating you right, you hate them for the rest of your life!

"We wanted so badly to help you with your chemical imbalance. You refused that help, too. We found many pills in your room after you left home at eighteen. You always promised you were taking them, but we know for a fact that you were not.

"I tried to teach you to keep clean. I showed you how to wash out clothing items when they became soiled due to your monthly periods. When we cleaned out your room, we found seventeen pair of bloody panties, hidden under your mattress.

"As we cleaned your room we found letters you wrote to your friends confirming the hate you felt toward us. It would be stupid for me to pretend we are not as different as night and day. Our life-style makes you nervous and your life-style makes all of us nervous. It should not be a surprise to you that the kids feel uncomfortable around you. You shouted at them constantly, teased them, scared them, threatened them, and, in general, made their lives miserable. Tattling and fussing are very typical among siblings, but your resentment showed more than just in a typical way. Do you think you are the only child in our family who suffered from tragedies and problems? You are not. The other children suffered from tragedies also. All that seemed to matter to you was that your life was miserable because of your bad attitude and unwillingness to cooperate even in a small way. You felt cheated, and I guess subconsciously you wanted to make everyone else as miserable as you were. You were not strong enough to rise above the situation and make the best out of your life. If you had risen above the circumstances, you would be a responsible adult by now.

"Your daddy got married the first time when he was eighteen. He never had to live with anyone or let anyone feed him. nor did anyone pay his bills. He worked at anything he could find and sometimes the working conditions were awful. He continually searched for better jobs. He was never late to a job, nor did he ever call in sick.

"As long as you are not able to put your past in the right perspective you will never be able to progress forward the way you should. Hate destroys, and if you do not stop hating us, eventually it will destroy you. Stop and think about your life, it was not all that bad.

"Whether you ever get over hating us or not is entirely up to you! I just wish you could remember the many wonderful things we have done for you. Even if we establish a better communication, neither your daddy nor I will ever be willing to let anyone take advantage of us, or expect material things or financial assistance from us. You were told that all of your life. You are an adult now. It is time to accept your adult responsibilities.

"We would like you to feel free to come over for a visit, but we still need you to call first because of the many activities that go on. I do not want to miss your visit because I am gone. I would be more than glad to rearrange my schedule if I just knew when you were coming.

"Do not get mad just because I have asked you to call first. I would like to think you want to be sensitive to the family's needs. If it is impossible for you to come on a certain day, do not get mad, just make different plans.

"Hurt feelings take time to heal. The kids that still live here will always be considered. They did not leave mad and they do not hate us. Even if we never capture a wonderful closeness, there is no reason for you to avoid calling, or for you to stay mad because things do not go the way you want them to.

"We would have been thrilled if you could have announced the arrival of your new baby yourself, instead of allowing us to hear about it through the announcement in the newspaper.

"Please stop telling people you won't call us because we won't talk to you. That is hogwash, and you know it! You chose not to talk to us. Stop twisting the truth around. Stop making your dad the bad guy. He loves you very much. We both love you and have tried to show you for years that we love you. It is you that can not talk to us, or express your love (if there is any) to us.

"We will always take our stand. We will always expect our children to grow up and be responsible adults. If they choose not to be responsible, we choose not to suffer for their wrong choices.

"You are not the only one who has experienced hard financial times. During my divorced time, my responsibilities were very difficult for me. It seemed like after I paid the bills and met my obligations toward the children, there was never any money left. I remember a few times doing without a meal myself so there would be plenty for my children. I never cheated my loved ones no matter how hard things got. I never asked anyone to pay my bills or buy my groceries or raise my children.

"We love you very much. We want you to become responsible for your own actions.

"We are very aware of how you feel toward us. I have asked each child to read this letter, and to tell me what they thought. Each child wanted you to understand how your actions have had a powerful impact on all of us. Each child, and your dad, said to mail this letter.

"There is a happy balance to everything. If you are overly affectionate, come for visits too often, and stay too long, then you have lost the balance needed for a good relationship. On the other hand, if you stay mad over little silly situations, never call, never visit, spread lies, and stay filled with hate, the balance had been lost again.

"It is our prayer that we can all maintain a happy balance in this relationship. We pray that none of us will remain overly sensitive about comments that are made and situations that occur that we do not understand. We gave you all we could while you were at home. We have other children to do for now, and we also owe ourselves some happiness.

'I am praying that you will read this letter with an open mind. For all these years you have only thought about your side of the story. Now Stacy, I am asking you to think about our side of the story and consider our feelings. I am asking you to focus on all the good, and put the sad, tragic times in their right place.

"You are an adult now, Stacy. Start expecting more from your own self and not so much from others.

"Our love,
"Mom and Dad"

I prayed before I wrote and mailed the letter. Now I had to trust God to intervene. I had to have faith that I had not misunderstood the Holy Spirit.

After I sent my letter, I became extremely nervous. Even though David and each child said to mail the letter, I was having second thoughts.

The day I mailed Stacy's letter I sat down to watch the evening news. Many times I avoided watching the news because it was so depressing, but for some reason I was watching it that day. A sad story was reported.

It seemed that a mentally unbalanced child went to his parents' twenty-fifth wedding anniversary party. He surprisingly opened fire and shot his parents, a guest, and himself. I felt sick. I thought for sure I had met my death. I jumped up and said, "I should not have mailed that letter. I am either going to get my head blown off or she is going to set fire to the house!"

David laughed at me, but I was really frightened by this story and began to remember how violent Stacy could be.

David sensed my genuine fear and said, "Honey, you have prayed about the letter, now you must have faith that God will take care of the matter."

I looked at David so strangely. He had reminded me of my terrible habit of doing things my way and not letting go and allowing God to take care of the situation His way.

"Thank you David, for reminding me that God will take care of this His way," I said.

20

Introducing *T. B.* and *Essie Maston*

Waiting for a response from the letter I had written Stacy was hard. I passed the time by reading. Among my favorite reading material is our church magazine. I was deeply touched by an article written about an elderly couple from Fort Worth, Texas.

T. B. and Essie Maston had been through a most unusual experience. Due to the misuse of forceps, their child was injured at birth and suffered from cerebral palsy.

T. B. Maston, professor at Southwestern Seminary in Fort Worth, and his wife Essie did not listen to the advice given to them by doctors and friends which was to place Tom Mc in a nursing home. Instead they prayed that God would give them the grace and strength they needed to outlive their son. The Mastons took Tom Mc with them everywhere, even to foreign countries when they went on mission trips. Tom Mc was an inspiration to others all around the world. Even though he could not talk, his happy disposition was a powerful influence.

The Mastons did not blame God for their grief, nor were they angry at the doctors. Mrs. Maston said, "The best way to handle grief is to face it."

I was so inspired by the Maston's story that I decided to call and talk with them personally.

Mrs. Maston answered, and I said hello to the sweetest voice I had ever heard. I introduced myself and instantly felt the warmth of a new friend.

Essie shared with me her experiences of raising an invalid son. The love she felt for her son was evident in her voice and through the illustrations she used. "It was hard," she told me. "Really hard!" She mentioned several routine methods of caring for her son. The things I might take for granted as a mother were not taken so lightly for the Mastons. Dressing Tom Mc and placing him in or out of his wheelchair were laborious tasks endured daily.

Friends repeatedly suggested that the Mastons' not even try to accomplish routine behavioral patterns. In spite of many discouragements Essie heard routinely, she kept a positive attitude and was determined to offer Tom Mc the happiest home environment possible. "It never entered our minds to take him out of our home to live. He was our son, and we would raise him. God gave us the strength." she said.

Through the Mastons' determination, Tom Mc learned to say "I" for yes and to bat his eyes for "no." Essie laughed slightly as she said, "Everyone told us we would never be able to toilet train Tom Mc, but we did!" She explained the routine of daily taking Tom Mc to the restroom at the same time of the morning. "It took hours every day," she said, "but finally Tom Mc understood what to do. I got tired of just sitting there with him for such long periods, but it was all worth it. When he became toilet trained, most of my problems were over."

The Maston's prayer continued to be, "Lord allow us to outlive Tom Mc. so we can care for him ourselves all of his life." *What thoughtful people,* I thought. They did not have a selfish bone in their bodies. Their only desire was to outlive their invalid son.

In November of 1987, Tom Mc died. Essie said they missed him very much and grieved like any parents who had lost a child. She said, "God is so good and answered our prayers to outlive Tom Mc." Tom Mc was sixty-one when he died.

What a story! What a wonderful illustration of unconditional love. I thanked Essie several times for sharing her story with me. What beautiful saints of God the Mastons were. They had been perfect examples of how the Holy Spirit can fill your life with unconditional love.

Essie proudly stated that she was eighty-nine and T. B. was ninety. "We have been married sixty-seven years," she said.

T. B. gave an illustration about a rubber band. He said he often showed his students how he flexed a rubber band between his thumb and forefinger, reminding them that a rubber band fulfills its function only when it is under tension. "Otherwise," he said, "it is just a flabby piece of rubber." I appreciated this illustration. It was a good example of how tension can bring progress.

I could only pray that the tension I experienced would be useful to me in my spiritual growth.

I knew I could not change the bad experiences or the failures of the past. I could apply those experiences to my future, though.

I occasionally come in contact with individuals who have or still have tragic illnesses or malfunctions of some kind causing great physical pain. In our modern day of miracle drugs and therapy, it is hard to imagine anything that is unable to be repaired.

One lady shared with me her experiences of participating in a stress clinic. A stress clinic teaches individuals to cope with a pain that can not be fixed or will not go away; a pain that surgery or a pill is unable to repair. This lady had learned to cope and endure her daily pain.

We all get very discouraged at one time or another. Life is full or problems and heartaches. I think it is important to fill our mind with positive thoughts.

One of the most inspiring stories I have ever heard was the one about a poor little black boy who lived in the slums of New York City. His father abandoned the family and the mother worked hard to make a living. Because of malnutrition and other problems, the little boy developed rickets in his legs. The family was not able to provide proper medical attention. Homemade crutches helped him walk until his legs were stronger. He grew up with a number of problems, but managed to work himself through college. Beating the odds, he began to show great potential in sports. His abilities in sports enabled him to achieve many goals. This person is O. J. Simpson.

He won the titles of All-American, the Heisman trophy, and All-Pro Running Back. The odds were against him but he overcame the obstacles by keeping his eyes on his goals.

This story can be applied to all of our lives, since we all have difficulties that get in our way.

We have heard many stories about alcoholics and their victories achieved with determination and self-control. I admire these people greatly.

I shall never forget watching a special on television starring Dick Van Dyke. He played the role of an alcoholic. His portrayal showed how an alcoholic's disease can affect loved ones and the family environment. Even though the program aired many years ago, I can remember being spellbound. I waited anxiously for his life to make a change. He put forth a sincere effort that involved various programs for alcoholics. He was miserable and so was everyone who was involved in his life. This was a good illustration of choice. The program ended with the alcoholic curled up on the ground underneath a bridge holding a whiskey bottle. It was a sad program, but very realistic. Many times our choices affect us and everyone's life that we come in contact with.

It was refreshing to remember these different situations; both good and bad. Life is a challenge for sure.

The most refreshing story was that of the Mastons'. Their example of unconditional love will remain with me forever.

21

A Positive *Response*

One evening when I returned home after completing routine errands, the children told me that Stacy had called. I stopped walking and breathing. I felt frozen and under my breath I whispered, "Thank goodness I was gone."

"What did she say," I asked.

My oldest daughter said, "She was real nice," She continued to tell me about the conversation, informing me of an apparently new attitude. "She said she would call you back."

Why was I trembling? I had nothing to be afraid of. It had been about a year since I had even heard Stacy's voice. Stacy did call back. "Hi Mom," Stacy said in response to my hello. For a second I could not speak, but then I quickly gathered my composure and made sure my voice sounded friendly and positive. We exchanged a few friendly words and then Stacy said, "I got your letter."

"You did? Is that good or bad," I asked tentatively.

Stacy said, "Well, it has taken me a few days to think it over." I was glad I sent a letter instead of trying to share my thoughts over the phone. I was right about Stacy needing time to reread the letter and think about the content. I sensed the tension in Stacy's voice. This call was hard for her, and suddenly I felt very proud that she had shown enough courage to call. I sympathized with her as she struggled for words. At the appropriate moment I thanked Stacy for calling.

"Thank you for having a sweet attitude. I know it must have been hard to call, and I appreciate your responding to my letter." With just those few words of praise, Stacy's voice changed to a more relaxed tone.

"I thought I was grown at eighteen, but I know now that I was not. I am still not grown," she said.

I almost fell over. Could this be Stacy talking? It was the first time I had ever heard her admit any kind of problem.

She continued by saying, "I really do not remember some of the things you mentioned in the letter, but I do realize how hard it is to be a parent. My children are eleven months apart and I feel very tired at the end of the day from taking care of them."

Throughout the conversation I recognized a wonderful change in Stacy's attitude. I also recognized some of her old disorders as she talked about her married life.

We talked for about an hour. She showed an interest in everything that had gone on for the past two years. She was interested in the children and all of their activities. It seemed strange to actually enjoy the conversation. I experienced a wonderful release of anger and bitterness. I felt that she had also released her bitterness.

As the conversation ended I said, "Stacy, thanks again for calling and for being so sweet." Then I said, "I love you, Stacy."

I could hardly believe I had spoken those words. I had not planned on saying those words, they just flowed out of my mouth like I was supposed to say them. My voice did not tremble. My tongue did not fall off. I did not faint or suffer from any discomforting feelings of any kind.

In the past I had told Stacy many, many times that I loved her but I think she knew I was going through the motions and just saying the "right stuff." On this occasion, my words were genuinely spoken. We can tell the difference in real sincerity compared to strained actions. It was a wonderful feeling to be able to speak without the usual strain.

The most wonderful surprise came when I heard Stacy say, "I love you too, Mom." Was I dreaming? Had I died and gone to heaven? Was this real?

Stacy called the next day to talk to her dad. David had been at work the first time Stacy called. He too sensed a sweeter spirit as they talked at length. Stacy told her dad that having children had really opened her eyes. David felt a real love from Stacy and our hearts were filled to overflowing at this new feeling of love we were both experiencing.

We made arrangements for Stacy and her family to come over for a visit. We felt excited about her visit instead of dreading it. It was such a nice experience to feel love instead of hate. I looked toward heaven and said, "Well Lord, am I finally learning my lesson?"

Within a few days of our phone conversation, Stacy and her family came over for our planned visit. We hugged each other when she came and my eyes were filled with tears.

She still had hygiene problems and her appearance still reflected the lack of confidence, but these traits no longer mattered. Stacy was home for a visit and we were glad to see her. I had finally learned how to love unconditionally. I could accept her now. For years I had tried to change her, but now I was learning to accept what I could not change.

Her baby was six weeks old and we loved on him and the one-year-old like they were long-lost friends. The one-year-old was walking now and full of energy! Stacy looked at me and said, "I think he is hyperactive."

"Well, at least you can fully understand the frustrations because you have been there," I said.

Stacy said, "Yes, I have and I have not completely outgrown it yet!"

I said, "You will be able to convince him to take his medicine since you understand how important it is."

Stacy said, "Yes I can, and if he does not believe me, I will just tell him to ask Grandma!"

"Just ask Grandma." That had a nice sound to it. Just ask Grandma and she will tell you how important it is to take that medication and receive counseling to avoid all of those psychological problems that can last a lifetime. Just ask Grandma since Grandma had to age and become a grandma before she learned the lesson of unconditional love.

David got the camera and took a roll of pictures.

We laughed and talked for hours. We got out the family pictures and I could see Stacy's blank look.

"Do you remember these occasions," we asked. She answered in a soft, stunned voice, "No..."

It was if she had proof of our kindness and was shocked at her misinterpretation of the way things really happened. Stacy realized for the first time that she had spent much time being mad. Being filled with anger had blinded her to our efforts. I stayed away from any negative comments or expressions. I was just thankful she could finally see things for the way they really were.

The children had been tense at first, but now they, too, were relaxed and seemed to be enjoying the visit.

Stacy and her husband still have lots of problems, but, then, who doesn't? God has taught me to accept,, understand, and love them just the way they are. Acceptance, understanding and love are the basic needs of any person; I was just now learning to give the basics.

Thank God, Stacy responded in such a positive way to my letter. Thank God I followed the leadership of the Holy Spirit and mailed the letter.

Stacy and I had changed together. Hate had been exchanged for love. This time I knew for sure that Stacy could feel that my love was real. I too, knew for sure that my love was real. There truly is not anything like the "real thing."

I found the Bible offered encouragement no matter what my circumstances were. I have learned to parallel the stories in the Bible to the situations in my life and amazingly there is always a story similar to my present episode in life.

I have gone to church since childhood and have listened to the same Bible stories over and over again.

I celebrated religious holidays like Christmas and Easter. At times my celebration became so festive that it diminished the meaning of Jesus' birth, death, and resurrection.

I was always certain that God created the world. I often looked up in the sky with awe as I acknowledged the magnificence of God's creation. I felt a sense of majesty when I gazed at some natural work of art like a mountain range, waterfall, lake, or canyon.

I have been overcome with emotion as I have witnessed and seen with my own eyes the miracle of childbirth.

Even though I have experienced admiration and wonderment, sometimes I forgot at times how real God is. At times God became a God who was just stuck way out there in heaven. Then I would have an amazing experience like this one with Stacy that reminded me that God is more than just an uncaring God.

I will never be able to analyze nature. I will never be able to factually prove that the Bible is true. I have no evidence that Jesus was born, died, and ascended into heaven. I do have faith, and I believe God sent His Son named Jesus to be born of Mary, a virgin. I believe He was crucified and suffered a cruel death on "an old rugged cross." I believe He arose victoriously from His grave; once dead and then miraculously alive again to ascend into heaven, leaving us His Holy Spirit to comfort each one of us.

What do all those beliefs really mean to me?

I had to meet God face to face, on a personal level. I had to experience His power and grace for myself. When I had a personal encounter then I knew how real God was.

Through my trials with Stacy, the Bible came alive with stories, examples, and illustrations to assist me.

How thankful I was for God's love that had taught me to love instead of hate.

22

Joseph and *His Coat* of Many Colors

A Bible story that left a lasting impression on me was the story of Joseph. Joseph was one of twelve sons. His father's name was Jacob. Jacob loved all twelve of his sons, but his favorite was Joseph.

In those days some items were very difficult to obtain. Jacob was fortunate to have the right colors of material to have a beautiful coat made for Joseph. The coat was brilliant because of the many colors of material used to make it.

Joseph was seventeen when he received this very special gift from his father When Jacob gave Joseph this beautiful coat, I can just imagine the reactions from his brothers.

Joseph's brothers were already jealous of the attention he had from their father, but his coat was too much!

Joseph is famous for his dreams, and many Christian teachers refer to Joseph as the dreamer. Joseph had a dream that made his brothers hate him even more. He dreamed that his brothers were binding bundles of grain in the field. His brothers' bundles bowed down to his bundle in Joseph's dream.

Having experienced the slanderous remarks between my own children, I can just imagine how Joseph's brothers reacted when they heard about this dream.

The Bible says Joseph's brothers scolded him unmercifully. Joseph had another dream. He dreamed the moon, stars, and sun bowed down to him. Joseph told his brothers about this dream, too! Even Joseph's father Jacob, asked Joseph if he really thought the family would bow down to him.

One day Jacob allowed Joseph to go to the field where his brothers were watching sheep. Joseph's brothers saw him coming and they plotting a way to kill Joseph. Their hate overpowered their sensible thinking and they wanted Joseph out of the family.

Reuben, the oldest brother suggested they not kill Joseph, but put him in a pit. They tore his beautiful coat off and smeared animal blood all over it.

About that time, some traders came by, so the brothers decided to sell Joseph to them as a slave for twenty pieces of silver.

When Joseph's brothers came home from the field, they put on a very convincing act for Jacob. "Look," they said, "we found Joseph's coat all torn and bloody." They explained a wild animal had probably killed Joseph.

Jacob looked at the coat and recognized it to be that of his beloved son Joseph. He cried, as he truly believed Joseph had been killed.

Meanwhile, the traders traveled to Egypt where they sold Joseph to Potiphar, the captain of the guard for Pharaoh.

Of course we will never know, but I tried to imagine how Joseph felt. He must have been deeply hurt that his brothers hated him enough to sell him. He must had been scared to death as he questioned his future welfare. The situation he was in looked very grim. God was with Joseph even during this bleak period of slavery because Potiphar put him in charge of all his possessions.

Potiphar's wife lied about Joseph and he was placed in prison. It is hard for me to even imagine how sad Joseph must have been. Rejection from his brothers, slavery, and now prison!

God continued to be with Joseph because the jail warden put all the other prisoners under Joseph.

Before long, the men in prison discovered Joseph's ability to interpret dreams.

One day two new prisoners came to Joseph. One man was Pharaoh's butler and the other was Pharaoh's baker. They explained their dreams to Joseph and God gave Joseph the meaning of the dreams. Joseph told the baker he would die and he told the butler he would get his job back. Joseph was right. The baker died and the butler got his job back.

Joseph asked the butler to remember him when he served Pharaoh again. The butler assured Joseph he would never forget him.

One day Pharaoh had a dream. He dreamed that seven fat cows walked out of a river. Seven thin cows came after the fat cows and ate them. Then Pharaoh dreamed seven thin ears of corn were on one stalk and they ate seven fat ears on another stalk. These dreams were very disturbing to Pharaoh. He called for wise men and magicians to tell him what his dreams meant, but no one could. Pharaoh's butler remembered Joseph. He told Pharaoh about meeting Joseph while in prison. Pharaoh was impressed and wanted to see Joseph immediately. Joseph was brought from prison and listened while the king told him about his dreams.

Joseph told Pharaoh that there would be seven years of good crops in Egypt and then there would be seven very poor years of no crops.

Joseph told Pharaoh he should look for a wise man to supervise the storing of extra grain during the seven good years to come in order to have grain during the famine.

Pharaoh recognized that Joseph's wisdom was from God and he was impressed that Joseph had interpreted the dreams so quickly. Because of Joseph's wisdom, Pharaoh made him the ruler of Egypt. The king gave Joseph his ring and many fine clothes.

Once a slave, then a prisoner, now a ruler. God was surely with Joseph.

For the next seven years, Egypt enjoyed the abundance of grain produced from the crops. Joseph very wisely supervised the storage of the abundance of grain produced from the crops. Joseph's dreams came to pass and just as he dreamed there was also seven years of famine.

Before long, small countries surrounding Egypt began to suffer. These countries had not stored the abundance of grain during the plentiful years.

Joseph's father Jacob and his brothers live in Canaan. Even now Jacob believed his son Joseph was dead. Years had passed since the betrayal of Joseph's brothers.

Jacob was concerned about his family during these years of famine. He sent his sons to Egypt to buy corn so they would have enough to eat.

Jacob's youngest son was Benjamin, and only he stayed behind as the others journeyed to Egypt.

When Joseph's brothers arrived in Egypt, they were directed to the Egyptian ruler. Joseph, the ruler, recognized his brothers, but his brothers did not recognize him. Joseph was loving and forgiving, even though his brothers had been so hateful to him during childhood.

He carefully kept his identity a secret until he was sure his brothers had changed.

As a test, Joseph accused his brothers of being spies. They pleaded with Joseph, explaining they had only come to Egypt to ask for corn.

Joseph told his brothers they must prove their character. He kept his brother Simeon, and sent the others home with the corn. He instructed them to bring Benjamin back and if they followed his instructions, he would release Simeon.

The brothers were sad to return home without Simeon.

With a heavy heart they explained to their father the conditions the Egyptian ruler had given them. Jacob was very sad, but allowed Benjamin to return to Egypt. When they all

joined together again in Egypt, Joseph's brothers bowed
down before him. Joseph's dream had come true.

Joseph continued to keep his identity a secret. He was
overcome with emotion as he saw all of his brothers. He had
his servants prepare a feast. Joseph's brothers could not understand why the ruler of Egypt offered them a feast, but
graciously enjoyed the wonderful meal provided for them. At
last, Joseph told his brothers who he was. They were
astonished, of course, I am sure they must have been surprised also because of Joseph's loving response to them. They
could all certainly remember the hate they demonstrated
toward Joseph by throwing him in a pit and selling him as a
slave.

Joseph planned a family reunion. His brother went to get
their father and share the good news.

As instructed, Jacob and his sons packed their belongings.
Joseph shared his good fortune with his family.

I visualized how excited Joseph must have been as he
waited for his family to join him. He had not seen his
father in many years and I could picture how happy Joseph
must have been. Joseph anxiously rode out in his chariot to
meet his family. He embraced his father and cried in his
arms.

Joseph experienced an awful and bitter childhood, but
through God's love he had forgiven his brothers for what they
had done.

God was always with Joseph even when it seemed like
Joseph was suffering alone. Joseph not only saved his family,
but he saved a whole nation.

God does not speak to me in dreams as He did Joseph. I
have never seen a heavenly vision or actually heard the voice
of God. God speaks to me through the Scriptures, and as I
worship Him in church. He speaks to me through unusual
events, spiritual leaders, and songs.

One Sunday night my youngest daughter was involved in a

children's choir presentation. The name of the musical was *The Song We Came to Sing.*

I knew my daughter had been practicing this musical for some time and I occasionally heard her practicing different songs included in the presentation. I was anxious to hear the entire musical.

The choir sang a number of songs but I could hardly believe my ears when the choir began to sing a song about Joseph called "Good for You."

This was one of those times I felt God speaking to me. Here are the words to the song.

Good for You

Now when Joseph was down in a deep, dark pit, he was surely as low as can be: and the Lord looked down there beneath the ground, and He helped poor Joseph to see. When you're down so low that the ground is up, and you don't understand all your bad, bad luck, just remember that Joseph had a down time too, and the good things for him can be good for you.

Joseph felt so said, 'cause he missed his dad, and he wanted to be with his friends, but he soon found out that without a doubt on the Lord he could always depend. When you're down so low that the ground is up, and you don't understand all your bad, bad luck, just remember that Joseph had a down time too, and the good things for him can be good for you.

Everybody knows how the story goes, and that Joseph had found a new home, and as you can tell, learned his lesson well, that the Lord takes care of His own. When you're down so low that the ground is up and you don't understand all your bad, bad luck, just remember that

Joseph had a down time too, and the good things for him can be good for you!

What a beautiful reminder to me personally. Some people might laugh if they heard me say that God spoke to me as the children sang. My faith allows me to believe that on occasions God does speak to us in our thoughts and through words or through songs.

Since I do not have spiritual dreams, or see visions from heaven, I will be glad to listen to God speak to me through these other ways.

23

The Best *Birthday* Party Ever

The warm sun beamed brilliantly through my bedroom window, gently waking me up. I smiled as I rolled over and hugged David.

There had been another time, eight years ago, very close to this same day, when I was meeting David's children for the very first time.

As I lay in bed watching David sleep, I reflected upon the past eight years. There had been struggles, heartaches, and problems, but through our love for God and our love for each other we had experienced a tremendous victory.

This beautiful spring morning brought yet another happy memory my way. Today was Stacy's twenty-first birthday. We were having a family birthday party today, and I could hardly wait to see Stacy and our grandchildren again.

David woke up and looked at me; we both smiled.

"This is a great day isn't it?"

"Yes," I said. We held each other for the next few minutes as we both silently recalled our struggles with Stacy.

After breakfast was over, I began cleaning the house and making preparations for Stacy's twenty-first birthday party. The children were eager to help. What a difference in each of our attitudes. We all chattered about as we waited for Stacy, her husband, and the babies to come.

I made a lemon birthday cake because I remembered it was

Stacy's favorite. I placed the birthday cake on the table and set the beautifully wrapped gifts around it.

Traditionally, birthdays were celebrated around the breakfast table. For years Stacy was awakened on her birthday by the sound of our voices singing "Happy birthday to you..." She bounced down the stairs and laughed with surprise at the festive display of gifts, cards, and a decorative birthday cake. For the past three years, there had been no celebrations and no Stacy! Now after three years, I was once again preparing the table in the traditional style. When I finished decorating, I stepped back and looked at the table. I smiled as I fought the tears. *Life sure can be painful,* I thought, *but this is a happy moment.*

I thought about Joseph and the family reunion he had. I remembered how God had turned his bad into good.

Stacy and her family arrived on time. As the car pulled up I watched for a few seconds as Stacy and her husband struggled with two children, a car seat, diaper bags, bottles, a baby swing, and baby toys.

How I remembered the days of being a young mother! At least Stacy was taking care of both children. Stacy and her husband still depended very much on the help of others, but at least their love for their children was obvious. I smiled again and walked toward the car.

"Need a little help?" I asked.

I took one baby and hugged the other one at the same time. As Stacy walked in, she looked at the table and smiled. "Wow! Just like old times," she said.

She hugged me and thanked me for the cake. When she had all the baby "stuff" situated we exchanged greetings again. As we sang "Happy Birthday" to Stacy, her eyes grew misty. "Why does it take so long to learn," she asked.

I did not have an answer for that question. It was the same question I had asked myself.

David lit the candles, and we all waited for Stacy to make

her wish and blow them out. Stacy looked around, smiled, and said, "I have already received my wish."

We all hugged Stacy as each of us told her we loved her. The birthday visit lasted all day. When the boys settled down for a nap, we sat outside in the beautiful warm spring weather. My children, Stacy's children, and our husbands were all preoccupied, so it was just Stacy and me sitting in the backyard.

Stacy was full of young mother stories. Occasionally, I laughed and said, "I remember that."

Stacy mentioned her one-year-old son having temper tantrums. I said, "Do you remember having temper tantrums until you were eighteen?" Stacy just looked at me as if she genuinely did not remember.

She talked about the jealousy the one-year-old demonstrated toward the baby. I sensed that I was not being inappropriate as I said, "Do you remember being so jealous of the kids that you sat on them until they could not breathe or dunked them until they thought they would drown?"

"No," she whispered.

It was at that moment I remembered reading that hyperactive children do not recognize that they are different. They sincerely are puzzled at other people's responses to them and they cannot see that their annoying habits are obnoxious to others. Their lives are filled with hundreds of incidents that occur daily. No wonder they cannot remember certain incidents that we, as parents, cannot forget.

Stacy really did not remember her irritating habits or the crises she caused. She expressed shock and amazement as we recalled other occasions that created crisis.

We enjoyed our day. The birthday celebration was a wonderful success. We enjoyed the grandchildren as we played with them. Stacy said thank you many times. What a wonderful, wonderful day we had as we celebrated Stacy's twenty-first birthday.

24

It Takes *Time*

There had been a time when it seemed it would be impossible to find the balance, take a tough love stand, be sensitive to all my children and to Stacy, as well as accept her disorder and express unconditional love. I realized David and I had finally accomplished the proper balance. It just took time!

Hebrews 11:1 says it all! "What is faith? It is the confident assurance that something we want is going to happen. It is the certainty that what we hope for is waiting for us, even though we cannot see it up ahead" (TLB).

Hebrews 12:7,9 says "Let God train you, for he is doing what any loving father does for his children. Since we respect our fathers here on earth, though they punish us, should we not all the more cheerfully submit to God's training so that we can begin really to live?" (TLB)

For many years I questioned if my efforts were even worth my time. It had appeared that my words of love, and my gifts and ideals were ineffective.

At times I questioned the cliché that "Love can change anything." It seemed for years my love had not changed one thing. As Stacy and I had visited she told me she was glad we had been so thoughtful to her during the past years. I was touched because I had never been sure she realized we were thoughtful.

Now, years later I was seeing the results of all my efforts.

Stacy asked, "Why is it you have to be an adult and have

children before you understand why your parents do certain things?"

With misty eyes I softly said, "Well... I just do not know."

Time, a painful thorn, and God's love, taught me patience and unconditional love. Time and God's love educated me by demonstrating through a stressful situation that my way was not always the right way.

Time and God's love taught me to adjust myself to what is and try not to adjust everything to my own desires. My opinions may be best for me, but that does not mean my opinion is always right for everyone else. Time and God's love changed my attitude toward Stacy and her in-laws.

Even though I choose not to personally endure the aggravation of allowing Stacy, her husband, and the two children to live in our home, I became very grateful to the mother-in-law because she had provided a temporary home for them. Without her assisting Stacy, I might not have had the joy of holding my grandbabies.

Stacy and her family are now living with the help of government assistance programs. They are no longer living with the in-laws. Their standard of living is not my choice, but time and God's love has taught me to accept their choice.

Stacy loves her husband and children, and they are happy. That is all that counts. The in-laws provided time for Stacy and her husband. This time allowed them to mature until they could arrange a living for themselves with the assistance of government programs.

As I share my own personal story, I realize there are millions who are struggling with the same frustration I felt. I referred to our situation as a "raging storm."

Those of us who suffer from problems that lack an immediate solution must learn to cope with daily pain and stress. Some might attend a stress clinic, others learn to develop strengths and endurance in other ways. God showed me how to be a more loving person and a less nagging one. He taught me to lean on Him in my weakness. He taught me how to accept what I could not change.

He taught us how to take a tough love stand without feeling ashamed or guilty. A tough love that would save our emotions and those emotions of our other children. He taught us unconditional love, and provided peace, strength, and understanding. He taught us that there was a balance to everything, and that balance is what we continually strive for even today.

Without the problems Stacy created through being hyperactive, I might not have acquired patience even today. I am proud to say I have finally learned to put on patience as part of my daily wardrobe.

In God's time I found a great teacher, healer, and provider.

The greatest gift for a hyperactive child is to know that he or she is loved. Just as great is for the parents to know that his child recognizes their love for him.

Epilogue

"Lord, teach me how to love my hyperactive child.
Quoting from a talk show my husband said, "Writers must be crazy!" He continued, "Writers stick their neck out, becoming vulnerable to every persons' reaction to what has been written. The reader's reaction might be angry and disturbed or happy and encouraged." I thought, "That sure is true." As a Christian writer I believe my inspiration comes from God. If I didn't feel His presence through countless rejections and negative responses from friends and loved ones, I never would have made it to first base.

Almost everyone experiences awkward situations and people that make them feel uncomfortable. Each one of us must handle our difficult situations in a way that best suits our emotional needs.

Six years have passed since I began writing the story of Stacy. David and I have been married twelve years. In the introduction of this book my pastor stated that the story of a hyperactive child is an unending one. This too is a fact with Stacy. We are sadly aware that Stacy divorced her husband and that she and her husband allowed Stacy's mother-in-law to legally adopt their children. We haven't heard or seen from her in years.

Stacy's mother-in-law deserves recognition for her compassion and ability to endure a very hard and trying situation. I admire her strength to cope.

My prayer is that my personal story will encourage each one who reads it. Each person must search for God's will in their own difficult situation allowing love and forgiveness to engulf the obstacles that come their way.